W9-AHA-672

THE FACE READER

THE FACE
READER

Discover Anyone's **Personality,**

Compatibility, Talents,

and **Challenges** *Through*

Chinese Face Reading

Patrician McCarthy

DUTTON

DUTTON
Published by Penguin Group (USA) Inc.
375 Hudson Street, New York, New York 10014, U.S.A.
Penguin Group (Canada), 90 Eglinton Avenue East, Suite 700, Toronto, Ontario M4P 2Y3, Canada
(a division of Pearson Penguin Canada Inc.); Penguin Books Ltd, 80 Strand, London WC2R 0RL,
England; Penguin Ireland, 25 St Stephen's Green, Dublin 2, Ireland (a division of Penguin Books Ltd);
Penguin Group (Australia), 250 Camberwell Road, Camberwell, Victoria 3124, Australia (a division of
Pearson Australia Group Pty Ltd); Penguin Books India Pvt Ltd, 11 Community Centre, Panchsheel
Park, New Delhi – 110 017, India; Penguin Group (NZ), 67 Apollo Drive, Mairangi Bay, Auckland 1311,
New Zealand (a division of Pearson New Zealand Ltd); Penguin Books (South Africa) (Pty) Ltd,
24 Sturdee Avenue, Rosebank, Johannesburg 2196, South Africa

Penguin Books Ltd, Registered Offices: 80 Strand, London WC2R 0RL, England

Published by Dutton, a member of Penguin Group (USA) Inc.

First printing, April 2007
10   9   8   7   6   5   4   3   2   1

 REGISTERED TRADEMARK—MARCA REGISTRADA

LIBRARY OF CONGRESS CATALOGING-IN-PUBLICATION DATA HAS BEEN APPLIED FOR.

ISBN 978-0-525-95000-4

Printed in the United States of America
Set in Horley
Designed by Richard Oriolo

For Elliot
whose face I love

CONTENTS

PART THREE: READING THE INDIVIDUAL FEATURES

AUTHOR'S NOTE

THE TAOIST PRINCIPLE OF THE Five Elements uses the metaphors of Wood, Fire, Earth, Metal, and Water to explain the relationship, interaction, and on-going change of everything in the Universe. The meaning of these Five Elements differs greatly from the Western definitions of the same words in that they each encompass the mind, body, and spirit aspects with which they are associated. To acknowledge this difference, these and other words associated with Taoism and Traditional Chinese Medicine are capitalized throughout the text of this book.

INTRODUCTION

MIEN SHIANG IS A NEARLY three-thousand-year-old Taoist practice of an art and a science that literally means face *(mien)* reading *(shiang)*.

If you know Mien Shiang (pronounced *myen shung*), you can determine anyone's character, personality, health, wealth potential, social standing, and longevity simply by looking at his or her face.

We live in an age of high technology. No matter the distance, we can communicate with one another directly and instantly by telephone, e-mail, fax, even by satellite. Yet, when something momentous occurs—such as a job interview or a marriage proposal—we nearly always have to do it face-to-face.

There's no doubt that communicating in person has a multitude of advantages over technology. In person, we can observe body language and read facial expressions to pick up on an attitude. Since there are many good con men and women who can instantly deceive you, however, you cannot rely completely on these observations. If you have ever played cards with a professional, or with my late Aunt Gertie, you understand the phrase *a good poker face*. A seasoned bluffer can easily manipulate a look or assume a studied posture to fool even the most observant person.

But face shapes, facial features, positions and sizes and shapes of each feature, lines, shadows, and other facial markings all tell the truth. They are foolproof signs, if you know how to read them. If you know Mien Shiang.

*Without wearing any mask we are conscious of, we
have a special face for each friend.*
OLIVER WENDELL HOLMES

HOW MIEN SHIANG CAN HELP YOU IN YOUR EVERYDAY LIFE

One of our most primitive instincts is the search for self-discovery. *Who am I?* This is the question that has occupied the thoughts and emotions of philosophers, poets, and dreamers everywhere, for all time. There are many fascinating and revealing paths on the journey of self-discovery. Mien Shiang can help you in your personal search for self. By looking in the mirror and studying your face, you can develop a profound understanding of your true nature. Identifying your true nature helps you first to recognize your inborn gifts and challenges, and then how to balance them to live your life, every single day, to its fullest.

Mien Shiang can also give you similar insights into everyone in your life. It can help you choose your true mate and find the best boss or hire a top employee. It can make all your family, professional, and social relationships smoother and richer. And, by knowing the significance of certain facial markings, Mien Shiang can help keep you healthy—it might even save your life.

THE ORIGIN OF MIEN SHIANG

Taoist monks were the healers, scholars, and advisers to the emperors in China. They were the first to use Mien Shiang, at least twenty-five hundred to three thousand years ago.

These monks used Mien Shiang much in the same manner as practitioners of Traditional Chinese Medicine do today, as a diagnostic tool to determine either an existing illness or an inherent susceptibility for particular body, mind, or spiritual ailments.

The scholars and advisers to the high-ranking officials used Mien Shiang to make direct decisions regarding personal integrity and honesty. We now live in a world of instant information. It takes only moments to find out nearly everything about anyone. But three thousand years ago, people could easily misrepresent themselves or their mission to the courts of the land. It might take days for a court emissary to reach a village only fifty miles away to confirm a messenger's story or purpose.

Consequently, emperors and other court officials relied on the opinions of their Mien Shiang advisers regarding the stranger's character, personality, potential, strengths, and weaknesses. They knew from experience that *the face is a mirror that records your past, reflects your present, and forecasts your future.*

From those earliest times the teachings of Mien Shiang were recorded by the monks and passed down from teacher to student. Then in 221 BC, Emperor Qin Shi Huang, first ruler of unified China, decreed all esoteric literature destroyed, including that which held the secrets of Mien Shiang.

The emperor was so convinced of the power of Mien Shiang that he ordered his own official portrait burned. He then commissioned a fabricated portrait of himself using a compilation of all the features Mien Shiang considered most positive. When his soldiers paraded through the far-flung villages and farmlands with this new portrait, the emperor's subjects saw him as a kind and benevolent ruler, not the power-mad tyrant that many claimed he really was.

Despite the emperor's attempt to destroy the teachings of Mien Shiang, it has lived on in China and other Eastern countries as an invaluable analytic tool and as an esoteric practice of determining personal and spiritual integrity.

In some ways, it's as easy today for people to misrepresent themselves as it was those thousands of years ago. While a good many people still live their entire lives not far from their birthplace, many others crisscross the globe, residing in a succession of cities, countries, and continents. Some of us change jobs as often as we change planes and trains. We are a society of multitalented people who enjoy reinventing ourselves every few years. While we do have instant access to certain personal and business information, that information is often tailored to conform to company policy, legal restrictions, or another's prejudicial experience with the person.

Through Mien Shiang you can do your own quick study of each person you meet to determine his or her basic nature, character, honesty, self-confidence, leadership abilities, stamina, loyalty, and potential.

HOW I CAME TO LEARN AND LOVE MIEN SHIANG

I stumbled upon Mien Shiang quite by accident. When I learned there was an ancient practice that could tell you nearly everything you wanted to know about a person by looking at his or her face, I was both amused and intrigued. Of course, I never imagined that years later I would be considered a leading authority on facial diagnosis. If anyone would have suggested that I would one day establish the Mien Shiang Institute and then create and teach the first-ever certificate program in the study of Medical Diagnostic Mien Shiang at a renowned university of Traditional Chinese Medicine; and further, present workshops to Fortune 500 executives and teams, traveling throughout the country to teach seminars to thousands who would become interested in Mien Shiang; why, I would probably have laughed myself silly. It's been a fascinating and absolutely joyful journey of study, love, and finally, of practicing and teaching what I have learned.

Several years ago, when I was young and newly married, my husband and I moved from New York City to Tucson, Arizona, where he was to begin his residency program in internal medicine. It was a great move for him, but I was apprehensive. I loved the bright lights, the exhilaration, the never-ending motion, and the surprise around every corner of the city. He disliked everything I loved about the city of his birth. Having been born and raised in staid and quiet New England, I no longer wanted that. Beauty and serenity were nice, but I couldn't imagine where the fun would be in that searing desert environment. (Later, after you have finished this book, if you come back and reread this description of me at this time of my life, I guarantee that you will easily be able to describe many of my facial traits and the Wu Xing element that determined my personality at that time!)

My background, and my intended future, was in filmmaking and writing. Since there wasn't a filmmaking community in Tucson at that time, I decided to hone my writing skills. What had attracted me to Tucson was the proximity of so many Native American tribes. I was born in Old Town, Maine, across the river from the Penobscot

Indian Reservation, where my father was born and raised. I was only six months old when my family moved to a small Air Force base in Vermont, where my father became the fire chief. The climate in the 1950s was not a very friendly one toward Native Americans, and my family was eager to put my father's ancestry behind them. It did, however, leave an empty place in my heart. Now that I was living amid so many Natives, in a more favorable time, I wanted to learn more about my heritage by writing a story about the Navajo, Pima, or Apache people.

After several false starts, I began a novel about a battle of water rights and the Apache tribes set in 1903 in Arizona. One morning I went to the Arizona Historical Society, where I was spending day after day researching life in the Old Pueblo, and saw an intriguing new exhibition mounted in the lobby. It was on the history of the Chinese in Tucson, from 1880 to the early 1900s.

Fifty or sixty sepia-toned photographs papered the narrow lobby walls. Photograph after photograph depicted Chinese immigrant men dressed in their pajama-like trousers and jackets, their long queues snaking from under round hats and making a straight black line down the middle of each of their backs. Young Chinese men posed awkwardly and unsmiling behind the counters of their chock-full general stores, or sat stiffly on wooden sidewalks next to signs reading WASH 5 CENTS. Others stared solemnly into the camera lens from their rickety and overflowing produce wagons.

I was pulled into the life behind those pictures as though I had somehow gone back home, to a place I'd been missing and mourning since before I was born. One picture especially pulled me, and I found myself holding my breath, staring at one single, tiny image of a young Chinese man among many others grouped tightly in front of a mercantile store on a dry dirt street. I know you, I thought. I know everything about you. I even know your name is Sing Cang. And then I fainted.

I had never fainted before, and I was frightened at first, but within a few minutes I knew that something profound had happened to me. I couldn't imagine, though, what it could be. That afternoon I changed the theme of my book from the Apaches and water rights to the anti-Chinese movement that was building in southern Arizona in 1903.

I went in search of some of the local Chinese families who could share their ancestors' stories of helping to settle old Tucson. No one wanted to talk to me. After a month of curt refusals I gave up. Another month passed and I received a call from the granddaughter of one of Tucson's first Chinese herbalists in the 1890s. Her widowed great-uncle had just arrived from Taiwan and was willing to talk with me.

Before they could change their minds, I was knocking on her door. I began to wonder what a newly arrived Taiwanese man could tell me about the Chinese in the Old West. Mrs. Lee brought me to the backyard, where Mr. Yi Ping Wong was sitting by the pool, dressed in a lightweight brown wool suit in the hundred-degree weather. Mrs. Lee told me he had put his suit on to be respectful to his guest and she couldn't get him to change. She served us iced tea and then left on some errands. So far Mr. Ping hadn't spoken a word. I asked him a few polite questions. He just smiled. Finally he pointed to my car in the driveway and then to both of us. After a few more charades, Mr. Ping and I went for a ride into the desert.

Sitting atop some jagged rocks overlooking a gorgeous sweep of saguaros and paloverdes, Mr. Ping finally spoke. "Tell me why you want to tell story about Chinese. You not Chinese." So I told him how my intentions to learn about my own culture had changed the moment I saw the picture of the young Chinese man in front of the store; I even told him about knowing Sing Cang's name, and fainting.

Mr. Ping thought for a few minutes. "Every day you take me for a ride and you tell me more about your story. I will tell you what is not good about it." I asked if he meant only from a Chinese point of view, or if perhaps he was a retired editor. He just smiled.

So every day we went to the desert and I told him about the story and he told me what was wrong with it. Which was pretty much everything. But I didn't care because he began to tell me stories. How he learned about Traditional Chinese Medicine from his father and uncles and grandfather while growing up in rural China, how his family fled to Taiwan during Mao's Revolution. How he was considered a master diagnostician, even better than his grandfather had been. Soon my book's character, Sing Cang, became a Chinese herbalist and master diagnostician in old Tucson in 1903.

Besides being a font of information on Chinese culture, Mr. Ping was quite good company. But there was something uncanny about the way he would tell me about myself. Things he couldn't possibly know, such as my medical history, my fears, how I behaved in specific situations. We never saw each other outside of our visits to the desert, and we didn't know anyone in common. It took a while before I realized that Mr. Ping made his remarkable diagnoses by reading my face. He had said so several times, but I thought it was a euphemism or a language barrier. He couldn't possibly mean it literally.

So began my study. For four years Mr. Ping and I would go to the desert and he would teach me Mien Shiang. At the beginning of our third year Mr. Ping announced that he was going back to Taiwan the next year to live with his nephew's family. It was too hot for him in Tucson. I suggested he might like it better if he traded in that brown wool suit for some Bermuda shorts and sandals. But he was determined to go back home. A few months later he arranged for me to meet an old friend and teacher from China who now lived in New York. That began my sporadic study with the creative and formidable Mr. Wong. (Every few months I would fly from Tucson, and then later from Los Angeles, where I had moved, to meet Mr. Wong at a little tea shop in Chinatown for my lessons.) It was at least two years into my informal study with Mr. Wong that I learned how hard Mr. Ping had lobbied him to take me on as an apprentice (of sorts). Women were not healers in China, and Mr. Wong didn't think they should be healers in America. At least not of Chinese medicine; Western medicine was not his concern. I don't think he would have taught me about face reading if he was not assured that I only wanted to learn so that I could write about it someday. I had long since abandoned my novel, but I was interested in writing about this strange and ancient diagnostic tool. I just wasn't sure how, or for whom. For once, my vagueness was my ticket to getting what I needed.

As I became more settled in the Los Angeles area, it was difficult to go to New York to see Mr. Wong. A relative of his knew a relative of a neighbor who led me to a few informal teachers in my area. Of particular note was Mr. Ling Wu Cheng in Monterey Park, California, who let me come to his herb shop on quiet Monday afternoons and ask him about face reading. For several years we kept up our casual tutelage, and then one day he told me he'd decided that I should teach Mien Shiang in the acupuncture schools because the American-educated acupuncturists who were coming to his shop didn't know about facial diagnosis. Mao's Cultural Revolution had banned the teaching of the esoteric arts in the schools, so the only healers who were learning the ancient teachings were those who were being mentored by family or personal teachers.

The idea seemed absurd at that time. I was neither a doctor of Traditional Chinese Medicine nor an acupuncturist. But Mien Shiang had become my passion, so I began to teach others in the same informal way I had been taught and mentored by my teachers.

Within a short time I was approached by so many healers of multidisciplines that I had to present workshops to include more students. Eventually, I formed a relationship with the founders of Yo San University of Traditional Chinese Medicine, who were impressed with my knowledge and ability to interpret my Mien Shiang readings.

When they asked me to create and teach the first-ever Medical Diagnostic Mien Shiang teaching program at the university, I was as convinced that no one else in the United States was as knowledgeable or qualified, so I happily accepted.

MIEN SHIANG: A HOLISTIC PRACTICE FOR MIND, BODY, SPIRIT

As you learn to read your face, you will see that the art and science of Mien Shiang is a holistic study and analysis.

Since Mien Shiang was first used as a diagnostic tool of Traditional Chinese Medicine (TCM), and since TCM is derived from the Taoist philosophy that claims no separation of mind, body, and spirit, it is impossible to separate those three integral aspects of yourself when you read your own, or another's, face.

In other words, you will not study your facial features and markings to determine only your personality traits, or only your emotional and spiritual well-being, or only your physical health. There is no separation. If you are in an emotional crisis, it will most likely show on your face. And where and how those signs appear on your face will alert you to specific corresponding physical and spiritual conditions that can become vulnerable as a result of that emotional imbalance. When one aspect of your being is out of balance, all will be imbalanced.

Sometimes it takes a while to get used to this holistic approach. In our culture we usually rely on an allopathic doctor (an M.D.) for our sore throat or burst appendix, then seek out a psychologist for our emotional suffering, and a priest, rabbi, minister, or other religious adviser for our spiritual crises. In Taoism, and therefore in Mien Shiang, since mind, body, and spirit are entirely interrelated and dependent upon the others, it will help you to start thinking holistically when learning to read your own face, as well as others' faces.

Of course, even though we approach face reading holistically, many times we focus on one of the three aspects more than the others.

I created the first Mien Shiang Certificate Program in conjunction with Yo San University of Traditional Chinese Medicine in Los Angeles, California, a few years ago. Its purpose was to educate students to use Mien Shiang as a critical diagnostic tool in their medical practices. Within that program, there is equal emphasis on the physical, emotional, and spiritual aspects of all symptoms, ailments, and diagnoses.

When I conduct my corporate and public seminars, however, I omit nearly all references to physical health, emphasize the emotional and personality characteristics that can be read on the face, and show how to use this knowledge to work and live together in a more harmonious and productive manner. Naturally, people in corporate groups want to know about their health, and I always agree to let anyone know privately if I see something that might suggest a health problem. (The consistent markings that I do see over and over in the corporate world relate to stress; but one doesn't have to be a face reader to know that!)

We will focus primarily on the characteristics related to mind and spirit and how being able to identify those traits in yourself and everyone around you will lead you to a more fulfilled life.

HOW TO USE THIS BOOK

Most of the books that I have seen on face reading jump directly to identifying the twelve or so facial features and listing the identifiable traits associated with each. While it is interesting to know that the size and shape of your nose reveals your ego, drive, and leadership potential, it is only part of the information we can gather from analyzing the nose, and all our features.

Since Mien Shiang is an ancient Taoist art and science based on Yin and Yang and the Five Elements, it is essential that we understand just what they are and how they are used in analyzing faces for character, personality, and spiritual traits before we begin to identify each feature's qualities. Equally important is having a comprehensive knowledge of the five basic Taoist personality types before learning which facial features are associated with each of the Five Elements, and what their specific traits are.

I have structured this book so that by the time you delve into the detailed characteristics of each feature in Part III, you will have an abundant knowledge of where those Taoist interpretations come from, and what they mean in relation to the Five Elements. When you have completed your own facial analysis, you will also understand your basic Five Element personality type.

THE ELEMENTS OF MIEN SHIANG

ONE

What Is a Face?

A FAVORITE QUESTION THAT I like to ask new students is *Why do we have a face?* I am usually met with a quiet sea of faces staring blankly at me. Everyone can articulate why we have facial features. We have eyes to see, noses to breathe and to smell, mouths to breathe and to eat, ears to hear and to balance, eyelashes to protect our eyes; but what about the face in its entirety?

RECOGNITION

The first purpose that comes to mind is identity. We recognize one another most often by our faces. True, most of us have distinguishing body shapes, or a distinct gait and posture. But how many times have you rushed up to greet a close friend, and when she turned to face you, you realized you had mistaken her for someone else? In a quick flash, you realized this the moment you saw her face. Of all the billions of people on this grand planet (nearly 7 billion, in fact) we each have our own distinctive look. Even identical twins are not truly identical.

I'm amazed and fascinated by this. Think of it: We all have a nose, and it's always in the middle of our face. We all have a mouth, and it's always right below our nose. We all have two eyes, two eyebrows, and two ears, and they are all in the same order and position as those of every other human being in the world. Yet we all look different, because we all are different. We are each unique and irreplaceable, and our faces reflect that every time someone looks at us.

COMMUNICATION

An equally significant role of our faces is communication. We express our feelings, our thoughts, and our moods on our faces. Along with body language our faces are integral in nonverbal communication. Just as tightly crossed arms indicate anger and noncooperation, a tensely set jaw and narrowed eyes convey those same emotions and attitudes.

Scientists acknowledge seven basic and universally recognized facial expressions: anger, fear, happiness, sadness, surprise, contempt, and disgust. Even babies as young as seven months old respond appropriately to facial expressions.

As effective as the face is at communicating emotions, it is equally capable of concealing or betraying true feelings. Facial expressions are influenced as much by culture as by biology. In China and in other Eastern countries, people have been practicing the art of Thick Black Theory for centuries. *Thick* refers to the face, and *Black* refers to the heart. To have Thick Face means you use your blank, expressionless face as a shield to protect yourself from the negative thoughts and influences of others, thereby never revealing your true feelings and emotions. To have Black Heart means you can still your heart, like cold, black ice, to become impervious to the dark and harmful thoughts of those who might wish you harm.

Our culture practices its own form of Thick Face when we smile at the boss who tells us we have to work late, again, or look surprised when Aunt Sophie gives us yet another rock-hard fruitcake for Christmas.

*　　*　　*

A couple years ago I was preparing a two-day seminar for the lead design team of a well-known Los Angeles advertising agency. A week before the seminar I arranged with the design manager to have my assistant go to the agency and photograph the design team while they worked and interacted. The only requirements were that they remove all jewelry, including rings and watches, and that they roll up their sleeves as high as they could.

On the morning of the first day of the seminar, the fifteen designers drifted into the company meeting room and found pinned to the easels and walls over a hundred cropped black-and-white photographs depicting only their hands. Some hands were photographed in extreme close-up, some were blurry with expressive motion, and some were lying still in quiet repose. Everyone flocked to the photos, laughing and having a great time guessing which hands belonged to whom. They were stunned when they realized just how much guessing was going on. At the end of half an hour there were many disagreements and contradictions. Several designers didn't recognize their own hands, not once but multiple times.

I suggested we take a quick break for the coffee and pastries awaiting us at the far end of the room. As we snacked and chatted by the pastry table, my assistant rolled in three long marker boards covered front and back with blank butcher paper. Wordlessly, he removed the butcher paper to reveal scores of five-by-eight close shots of the designers' faces that he had taken the week before. The recognition was instant. Even if the picture was blurred or angled or the lighting was poor, the artists recognized themselves and each other in the small images from across the room. When we all gathered around the face photographs, I went from shot to shot and asked what emotion was being expressed in each one. The designers were at least 90 percent in agreement for each photograph.

Since the designers were visual artists, it's not surprising that they scored so high at recognizing the emotions associated with the facial expressions. But most people are accurate at least 75 to 80 percent of the time.

After they had so successfully identified the emotions in the photographs, I asked everyone to sit down and to introduce themselves to me, but not to tell me anything about themselves. Let me tell you all about you over these next couple days, I suggested.

Following our introductions, I gestured to a dark-haired woman of about twenty-seven and the man in his midthirties with the clean-shaved head sitting next to her. "When we went around the room, Marlena and Richard introduced themselves, and now that I look back at this side of the table, I recognize them," I said, moving closer to them and looking directly from one to the other. "I recognize their *faces*. And I can tell by their expressions that Marlena is a little embarrassed by my attention, and Richard is amused. Am I right?"

Marlena blushed a little bit more as she nodded, and Richard's grin got bigger as he acknowledged that I was indeed correct.

"Is there anyone in this room who does not recognize Marlena's and Richard's faces? Or couldn't interpret their expressions?" I asked. All thirteen of the other artists in the group said they had no trouble recognizing their coworkers' faces, nor their embarrassed and amused expressions.

"Good. That's what we expect. Now, let's do a little Mien Shiang, some actual reading of their faces. Do you think that I can tell you, simply by looking at Marlena's and Richard's faces—by quickly observing the shape of their faces, and the size, shape, and position of each feature, as well as their lines and markings—which one is extremely practical and efficient, and which one is a big risk-taker?"

A surprised laugh erupted from the group as though I had just referred to a private joke that I couldn't possibly be in on.

Patti, a woman with a glittering strand of semiprecious gems wound artfully around her long neck, spoke up. "Since this seminar *is* about reading faces, you're probably going to tell us that you can see all sorts of things," she said with friendly skepticism. "But we're laughing because you just happened to pick the two traits that fit these two people perfectly!"

"Oh, no, it wasn't by chance," I said. "It's because I really do know how to *read their faces*. I know by Marlena's long, narrow nose and her high-arched eyebrows that she is exceptionally efficient and practical, and the size and shape of Richard's ears tells me that he is a great risk-taker.

"And I know by taking only a quick look at your face, Patti, that your biggest problem at work is that you scatter your energies." I smiled as Patti's eyes widened with confirmation. "Do you want me to tell you more?" I asked, even though I knew everyone had already agreed to being "read" prior to the seminar.

"Absolutely, tell me everything," she said, opening her arms wide as though to say she was a book waiting to be read.

"Well, just one more thing for now: I can tell from your eyebrows that even though you are the first one to offer help to your teammates, you have a very difficult time asking for help for yourself, and that means you often fall behind, even in trouble-free projects."

"This is amazing," Patti said, shaking her head in wonder, while the others were substantiating my quick reading of their teammate.

"It is amazing," I agreed. "And by the end of this seminar, you'll be able to read faces, too. By the end of today, even."

I love that moment when someone's face lights up, suddenly realizing that Mien Shiang really works!

Many readers will flip through the first pages and go to Part III right away to learn what the associations are with their own high cheekbones, or what their boss's long, rectangular face means, or what the lines around their new romantic partner's eyes indicate. If it's your nature to start at the end, go ahead and have fun. Then come back and start at the beginning so you may fully understand the fascinating and revealing intricacies of Mien Shiang. Find out through this ancient art and science which features and markings on your face you have inherited from your parents and ancestors, and which ones you have acquired through your own life experiences. Learn more about Yin and Yang and the Five Elements and how to use these Taoist modalities to build and stretch your knowledge until you can read not only certain fundamental facial traits, but hundreds of personality and behavioral characteristics associated with your basic nature. When you apply that same knowledge to reading other people's faces, you will be amazed at how much easier it will be for you to have more profoundly fulfilling and deeper relationships with anyone and everyone in your life.

TWO

The Five Taoist Principles of Mien Shiang

FIVE BASIC TAOIST PRINCIPLES OF *Harmony, Entirety, Qi, Yin and Yang,* and *Wu Xing* (the Five Elements) comprise the study and interpretation of Mien Shiang. The principles of Yin and Yang and of Wu Xing are the core of Taoism, and we will keep referring back to each of them in greater detail and depth as we broaden our knowledge of face reading.

THE PRINCIPLE OF HARMONY

The Taoist Principle of Harmony applies to Mien Shiang in that the more balanced the facial features, and the more complementary and integral each feature is to the other, the more favorable the potential for good health, good luck, and prosperity.

THE PRINCIPLE OF ENTIRETY

Though Mien Shiang means literally *face reading*, the full analysis requires attention to the entire presentation of the person. Just as doctors of Traditional Chinese Medicine and Western allopathic medicine who use Mien Shiang as a diagnostic tool are not going to ignore the rest of the person, nor should you in your evaluations.

One's body size and shape, feel, posture, gait, and movement, as well as the sounds of one's voice, one's laughter and cry, even one's expressions, contribute to the final assessment of each person.

THE PRINCIPLE OF QI

Qi (pronounced *chee*) is the life force, or spiritual energy, that is present in everything in the universe, including every living being. When practicing Mien Shiang, we assess the state of Qi in a person's body and face.

That might sound a bit esoteric or perhaps even impossible to do, but with a little practice and attention it's actually quite simple. Many of my students don't believe me when I first tell them that each of us has Qi, and that by careful observance they can not only "see" the Qi in each other, but they can perceive in which direction it is—or isn't—moving. So I bring a few people to the front of the room and we look at them. We focus on their stance, their breath, and their general physical energy. And sure enough, someone will quickly notice that each of the people standing before him actually "feels" different from the others. And that difference has an energetic quality about it, and that energy does move—sometimes quickly, sometimes hardly at all, and sometimes up or down or maybe even in a soft circular motion. Soon, most can detect the Qi, and the group is nearly always in agreement on the Qi's movement and direction. If you have not already begun to observe the energy in others, start now, and you'll be surprised how quickly you will "see" the Qi.

THE PRINCIPLE OF YIN AND YANG

The principle of Yin and Yang is the root of Taoism. It is the belief that everything within the universe is one of two opposites, and that each opposite produces the other. Yin and Yang are constantly seeking a balance, as well as demonstrating the obvious need for an opposite for any one thing to exist. If we did not have dark, we would not know that there is light; if we never experienced sorrow, we would not know the wonder of joy. Yang is represented by Heaven, and Earth, being Heaven's opposite, is Yin. Yang is day, Yin is night. Yang is hot, Yin is cold. The comparisons are never-ending.

YIN AND YANG TRAITS

YIN	YANG
dark	light
quiet	action
earth	heaven
moon	sun
cold	heat
female	male
absorption	penetration
even	odd
holistic	logical
intuitive	rational
creative	factual

Using Yin and Yang to Read the Face

One of the first things we do when we read a face is see how well-balanced it is in terms of Yin and Yang. Is there symmetry between the Mountains and the Valleys of the face? The Mountains are the hard, sharp, and stable parts of the face, and we call them the Yang areas. The Valleys, or the soft, fluid, rounded, and changing components of the face, are the Yin areas.

Therefore, the hard bone structures such as the forehead, brow bones, cheekbones, chin, and jaws are Yang. The softer cartilage features—such as the ears and nose, which continue growing after puberty; the tissue areas such as those padding the cheeks and chin and nose tip; and the mouth and the eyes, which are soft and fluid—are all Yin features.

A famous person with a predominantly Yin face is Renée Zellweger, who has plump, soft lips and a fullness around her eyes and her upper eyelids. Her cheeks and round chin also appear supple, as though they have a little padding over the bone.

Marilyn Monroe also had soft Yin features: a soft, full mouth; a round, wide nose tip; a round, soft chin; pliant cheeks; and heavy-lidded eyes.

Oprah Winfrey is another great example of a Yin face, with her prominently round cheeks and nose tip, her full, soft mouth, and the softness around her eyes.

Lance Armstrong has a model Yang face with his long, hard nose; wide, thin mouth; high cheekbones; strong, hard chin; and strong brow bones. Although Arnold Schwarzenegger has a bit more of a fleshy face than Lance Armstrong, his features are also predominantly Yang, especially his brow bones, nose, cheekbones, and chin.

Many people have a combination of Yin and Yang faces. Think of the star of the television series *The Sopranos*, James Gandolfini. He has a soft, wide Yin nose; thin lips that are sharp and Yang; Yin padding on his cheeks; a full chin; a high, "hard" Yang forehead with prominent brow bones; and Yang ears with hard cartilage and almost no lobes. With all of these Yin and Yang characteristics, James Gandolfini is an interesting balance of energies, as so many of us are.

Yin and Yang are always changing, just as our faces change many times and ways throughout our lives. How often have you seen old photographs of people you know and yet not recognized them? As we mature, some features such as our nose may lengthen and widen while other features such as our mouth and eyes might shrink or sink. Stress and grief may temporarily cause our entire face to sag and wrinkle or turn ashen. And great happiness gives us a glow and literally perks up and plumps out our features.

Someone asked me recently if the ideal face is a perfectly balanced symmetrical face. The answer, of course, is only if you are striving for a perfectly balanced life of mind, body, and spirit. On the other hand, complete balance is not ideal for everyone. The more Yang you have, the more of a doer you are—out there in the world leading, pushing the boundaries, getting things done. If you have more Yin, you are more inward, more imaginative and contemplative, with the gift to think things through before acting. The excess-Yang and the excess-Yin personalities are each capable of "going deeper" in their own ways. They often make excellent partners, each providing an insight and an expertise that the other would never gather on his or her own. If each of those people were perfectly balanced, they might only skim the surface of each situation rather than experience their own unique highs and great depths.

*   *   *

A few years ago my friend Paul Linke, a talented actor and writer, lost his beloved thirty-seven-year-old wife to breast cancer.

About a week after Francesca's death I made plans to join Paul for coffee at our local meeting place in Venice, California. It was a quiet midmorning at the Rose Café as I waited for Paul. He was usually punctual, but I could understand how difficult it must have been for him to get his two young boys off to school and his one-year-old baby girl to the babysitter and still be on time. As I waited for Paul, an old man stopped near my table and looked at me with a disarming directness. I smiled briefly, then looked down at my newspaper, not wanting a conversation with the stranger. Suddenly I realized the old man was my friend Paul. I had been out of town and had not seen Paul for several weeks, and in his sorrow he had aged two decades in ten days. I will never forget the grief lines running down from under his eyes, cutting deeply into his sunken, drawn cheeks. There were so many more lines—shooting out from around his eyes, circling and pinching his mouth, furrowing his forehead. His face was as gray and thin as the overcast day.

Within a few weeks, as Paul's grief abated somewhat, so did the harsh grief lines on his face. His color returned and he lost the slackness in his lower face. Slowly, he began once again to look like a healthy forty-year-old man.

A couple years later Paul wrote and starred in a brilliant one-man stage show, *Time Flies When You're Alive*, chronicling his relationship with his late wife, and his sad loss. It was later made into a film, and I urge you to rent this heartbreaking and achingly funny story. Note the changes in Paul's face as he shares the joys and heartbreak of his adventure with life, death, and life once again. A couple of times, as he relives his grief, those long, deep lines suddenly reappear on his cheeks. By the end of the film, as Paul reassures his audience, and himself, that his life has come full circle, once again full of wonder and love, you can see the grief lines literally disappear, and the fullness of joy reflected on his face. The imbalance of the Yin and Yang in Paul's life was reflected on his face, just as it is on most of our faces throughout our constantly changing journey through life.

Every person comes into the world with a little more Yin or a little more Yang, and that balance will shift throughout life. For some, the shifting of Yin and Yang will be like a boat rocking gently on a lake; for others, it will be like a wild ride on a stormy sea. Our faces reflect these ever-changing Yin and Yang balancing acts from the beginning to the end of our lives.

THE PRINCIPLE OF THE FIVE ELEMENTS

The early Taoist philosophers used the metaphor of the Five Elements, *Fire*, *Earth*, *Metal*, *Water*, and *Wood*, to explain the relationship, interaction, and ongoing change of everything in the universe. The metaphor was used first to describe the evolving cyclical seasons by dividing the year into five segments, or phases—spring, summer, late summer, autumn, and winter—and then assigning each season an element that would help to explain the nature of the seasonal changes and interactions, including the interrelationships among seasons. Even the most humble peasants could relate to these metaphors and their specific associated traits in order to effectively farm their land, fish their lakes, and prepare their homes for the inevitable revolution of climate. These same associations were later applied to every single aspect of life, whether it was physical, mental, or spiritual.

SEASON	ELEMENT
Spring	Wood
Summer	Fire
Late summer	Earth
Autumn	Metal
Winter	Water

Each of the Five Elements affects the others in either a positive or negative way. Fire generates Earth, Earth generates Metal, Metal generates Water, Water generates Wood, and Wood, completing the circle, generates Fire. This *Generating Cycle* is the sympathetic cycle of harmony and support, meaning that each element receives support from the previous element and gives support to the following element.

THE GENERATING CYCLE

Fire generates Earth
Earth generates Metal
Metal generates Water
Water generates Wood
Wood generates Fire

The *Controlling Cycle* is the nonsympathetic cycle of dominance wherein each element is controlled by one other element, which is recognized as its stronger counterpart. Fire controls Metal, Metal controls Wood, Wood controls Earth, Earth controls Water, and Water controls Fire.

THE CONTROLLING CYCLE

Fire is controlled by (put out by) Water

Earth is controlled by (shored up by) Wood

Metal is controlled by (melted by) Fire

Water is controlled by (contained by) Earth

Wood is controlled by (cut by) Metal

This continuous cycle of mutual generation and control sustains and balances the Universe.

THREE

Using the Five Elements and Their Associations to Read the Face

IN MIEN SHIANG WE USE the Five Elements to describe individual personality types. Our faces reflect our dominant characteristics and traits, giving us instant awareness of our basic constitutions for health, emotionality, and spirituality, as well as personality.

It is the shapes, sizes, colors, and markings on our faces that determine which of the Five Elements best define our nature and personality.

When you become familiar with the emotion, color, shape, body organ, sense organ, sense, direction, climate, season, and expression associated with each of the Five Elements, you will begin to see how those traits reflected on your face define your Five Element personality type.

ELEMENT	FIRE	EARTH	METAL	WATER	WOOD
Emotion	joy	worry	grief	fear	anger
Color	red	yellow	white	black/blue	green
Shape	peaked	square	round	amorphous	rectangle
Body organ	heart	stomach	lungs	kidneys	liver
Sense organ	tongue	mouth	nose	ears	eyes
Sense	speech	taste	smell	hearing	sight
Direction	south	center	west	north	east
Adverse climate	heat	moisture	dryness	cold	wind
Season	summer	late summer	autumn	winter	spring
Expression	laugh	sigh	weep	groan	shout

*Yesterday is ashes; tomorrow wood. Only today
does the fire burn brightly.*

ESKIMO PROVERB

When you have learned to read your face, you might discover that you have pre-dominately *Fire features*. If so, we can be fairly certain most of the following will be true: Your dominant emotion is joy, your skin tone is pink or reddish, you have an oval-shaped face, your tongue is often wagging in excited speech, most of your ail-ments are related to the Qi (energy) of your heart either physically, emotionally, or spiritually, your laughter is frequent, the south is your significant direction, and you are most affected by heat and summer.

If you find you have mainly *Earth features*, your dominant emotion is worry, your skin tone is yellowish, you have a square-shaped face, your mouth is prominent and you are comforted by tasty food, most of your ailments are related to the Qi of your stomach either physically, emotionally, or spiritually, you have a singsonglike voice, like a soft sigh you are most drawn to the center, and you are most affected by mois-ture and late summer.

When you have mostly *Metal features*, your dominant emotion is grief, your skin tone is pale or delicate, you have a round face, your nose and sense of smell are both sharp, most of your ailments are related to the Qi of your lungs either physically, emotionally, or spiritually, your voice is a little tight as though you are trying not to weep, your significant direction is west, and you are most affected by dryness and autumn.

If you find you have mainly *Water features*, your dominant emotion is fear, your skin tone has a tinge of blue, your lower cheeks are full and project a fluid, amorphous shape to your face, your ears and hearing are sensitive, most of your ailments are related to the Qi of your kidneys either physically, emotionally, or spiritually, the ends of your sentences trail off sounding like little groans, the north is your significant direction, and you are most affected by the cold and winter.

If you have mostly *Wood features*, your dominant emotion is anger, your skin has tones of green, you have a rectangular-shaped face, your eyes and sight are focused and intense, most of your ailments will be related to your liver, the east is your significant direction, and you are most affected by the wind and spring.

These qualities might not all fit your Fire, Earth, Metal, Water, or Wood personality—but I'm betting most will.

Remember when you are evaluating personality types for yourself and others to keep in mind the inherent supports and conflicts among the elemental types.

For instance, if you are a Fire element type, then you would normally feel most comfortable and supported by a person who is a Wood element. In turn, you would be especially supportive to Earth element people. Those with whom you might have difficulty are Water element people, since you often feel that they are so unresponsive to your high energy that it is as though they are "putting out your fire." Though sometimes, when you're feeling a bit frenzied or out of control, you might just welcome a little "watering down."

WHAT DETERMINES OUR FIVE ELEMENT CONSTITUTIONAL TYPE

No one comes into the world with a perfect balance of the Five Elements. Traditional Chinese Medicine teaches us that for a myriad of reasons, from inherited traits or genetics to stresses incurred by the mother during pregnancy or delivery, each of us is born with more of an imbalance, or a weakness, of one of the organs associated with the Five Elements. That organ imbalance, however slight or pronounced, will adversely affect our physical, emotional, and spiritual constitution for our entire lives. As we saw in the Wu Xing/Five Elements Associations chart, if the organ affected is the heart, you are considered a constitutional Fire element type; if the organ is the stomach, you are a constitutional Earth element type; if the organ is the lungs, you are a constitutional Metal element type; if the organ is the kidneys, you are a constitutional Water element type; and if the organ is the liver, you are a constitutional Wood element type.

That does not mean that all people who are of the Metal element type, for example, will have lung disease or be in a constant state of grief, or that all Water people will be troubled by their kidneys and be debilitated by fear. It does mean, though, that there is more of a chance that during extreme vulnerability the ailments and emotions associated with these organs will present related challenges in life.

It is important to remember that our challenges are most often our gifts as well. Many of us learn life's most important lessons through our challenges. Our lives are enriched beyond imagination after having gone through these rough spells.

It is a wonderful gift to know the strengths and limitations associated with our constitutional natures. It helps us to choose the best lifestyle, diet, and exercise to nourish and strengthen our imbalances.

I realize that this theory of living might sound strange or even a little daunting to those of us accustomed to a more Western approach. In this practice we are referring to a system of balances, and since everything is always and constantly changing, complete balance is never possible. Besides, since everyone has at least one dominant challenge in his or her life, isn't it better to know what yours is early on so that you can prevent disharmony and lead a healthy, happy, and stable life?

A FIVE ELEMENT BALANCING ACT

I am frequently asked if it should be our life's goal to achieve a complete constitutional balance of the Five Elements. My answer is always a resounding no. It is impossible to do, and to dedicate our lives to achieving the impossible would be frustrating indeed. To attempt this would create illness of mind, body, and spirit.

If we were all perfectly balanced, we would all be completely alike; or enough alike that we would bore each other to distraction. It's those little kinks in our personalities—the challenges that confound us, the honest mistakes we make—that endear us to our loved ones and friends. Our imperfections make us insightful, brave, strong, unique, and lovable. Always strive to grow, to learn, to teach, and to love, and you will be as balanced a person as you can and need to be.

FOUR

Five Element Personality Tests

THE FIVE ELEMENT PERSONALITY QUIZ

The following twenty multiple-choice questions are designed to help you to determine your dominant personal elements of Wood, Fire, Earth, Metal, and Water.

You might find that you are overwhelmingly one element, or a combination of two, or even three. You might also discover that you are quite deficient in one or two of the elements. Hopefully, this knowledge will give you greater insight into your behaviors, natural gifts, and challenges and illuminate why you make some of your choices in life. Use this wisdom to nurture those gifts and to appreciate and develop creative new ways to recognize and face your challenges.

To get the best results from this test, consider each of the twenty questions and then choose one of the five answers that best describes your behavior or personality in that situation. It's tempting to choose the answer that illustrates whom you might like to be, or how you would prefer to behave, but to help yourself find your true element, be introspective and honest in choosing your answers. For instance, when you have a question such as number thirteen, where you are asked to consider what kind of tree best fits your personality, choose the one that represents who you actually are, not the tree that you would prefer to be like.

Some of my students and clients have told me that if they find that they identify with every single answer, or cannot decide between a couple of them, they ask themselves which answer their family and friends would choose for them, and that usually gives them helpful insight.

THE FIVE ELEMENT PERSONALITY QUIZ

1. My movements are
   a. focused, fast, direct
   b. spontaneous, animated, scattered
   c. slow, deliberate, plodding
   d. precise, composed, rigid
   e. swaying, sensual, meandering

2. I could most be described as:
   a. a rooted tree
   b. a flickering flame
   c. a warm stone
   d. an elegant diamond
   e. a flowing stream

3. In an emergency situation such as an accident, if I am in a group, my role is most likely to
   a. immediately begin a rescue
   b. march right to the heart of the fray and provide loving comfort to the victims
   c. though overwhelmed, give support to whoever needs it most
   d. quickly and efficiently take care of details like calling 911 or giving directions
   e. step back and assess the situation, especially the safety issues

4. I have a weekday doctor's appointment and have a full schedule at work/home; the doctor is late. I
   a. get angry and let the staff know it
   b. use my humor to entertain myself and pass the time

c. become worried and agitated

d. wait a reasonable amount of time, then if I must leave, make another appointment

e. become impatient, especially since I have an issue with being late

5. My ideal first date would be

a. something sporty, active

b. anything fun with lots of talking and laughing

c. a movie and a pizza at my cozy neighborhood café

d. dinner at a fine restaurant, or the arts

e. dinner at a small café, and a meandering walk talking about poetry or politics

6. My sweetie and I are celebrating our first year together. I'd love to

a. go on a kayaking trip

b. go to a B&B in the wine country and have lots of romance and laughs

c. stay home, go to the movies, putter together in the garden

d. go to an upscale resort and enjoy the local museums and end with a quiet, elegant dinner

e. go anywhere where we can sleep late, meander all over town all day and night taking our time and just seeing what happens

7. I am going to a business conference where spouses or loved ones are welcome. I

a. would rather go alone and concentrate on my work in order to make new business connections

b. can't wait—it'll be great fun for us both to do something new and meet new people

c. like to have my loved one come with me to give me confidence and comfort in social situations

d. think that's lovely—he/she provides a wonderful excuse not to have to spend too much time with the others in the evening

e. would like my loved one to see me in my element

8. I'm on my way to spend a pleasant couple of hours alone at a favorite place when I get stuck in a traffic jam, without my cell phone. I am most likely to

a. get angry, blow my horn

b. turn up the radio and sing along; smile and shrug lightheartedly with those stuck next to me

c. worry that there might be an accident or something else bad up ahead

     d.   stay cool knowing this, too, shall pass

     e.   use the downtime to daydream and think

9.   When my loved one is away for several days on business, I

     a.   use the free time to work out, catch up on work

     b.   send them fun, loving messages; have fun with my friends

     c.   worry if they're all right, especially if they don't call or e-mail me frequently

     d.   am fine—I miss my loved one, but I don't need to express it; besides, I don't want to distract him/her from work responsibilities

     e.   use the time to do quiet, sensual things like take a long bath, have a massage, read

10.   Giving a dinner party is

     a.   good for impressing the boss or new clients

     b.   fun, fun, fun

     c.   a lot of work, overwhelming

     d.   best when well planned

     e.   a wonderful way to bring together interesting people who enjoy good conversation and friendly debate

11.   If a friend betrays me, my nature is to

     a.   confront him or her, perhaps even yell or retaliate

     b.   be heartbroken and blame myself even when I know it's not my fault

     c.   be sick to my stomach, then try to understand, even patch things up

     d.   cut him or her off

     e.   retreat, intellectualize, and then be determined to seek true justice and fairness for both of us

12.   If I were water, I would be described as

     a.   raging, rushing rapids

     b.   the mist that scatters and dances at the bottom of a beautiful waterfall

     c.   a comforting pond

     d.   a cool, beautiful glacier

     e.   a flowing river

13.   If I were a tree, I would be described as a

     a.   redwood

     b.   cherry tree in bloom

     c.   Douglas fir

    d.   winter birch

    e.   magnolia

14.   If I were fire, I would be

    a.   raging

    b.   playful

    c.   warming

    d.   contained

    e.   mysterious

15.   If I were made of earth, I would be described as

    a.   a mountain

    b.   sparkling desert sands

    c.   clay

    d.   fine, cool, white sand

    e.   a sand dune

16.   I am attending an office seminar where my office team will have to role-play assigned scenarios. I

    a.   think it's ridiculous and will do everything in my power not to participate

    b.   try to add some flare and entertainment

    c.   am willing to try, as long as it's not embarrassing to anyone on the team

    d.   would rather help plan or direct than perform

    e.   think it might be an interesting way to find out who each of my teammates really is, deep inside

17.   When someone looks me in the eye, I think they are responding to my

    a.   intense eyes

    b.   sparkling eyes

    c.   warm eyes

    d.   cool eyes

    e.   dreamy eyes

18.   When my friend is in an emotional crisis and asks me for good advice, I

    a.   expect my friend will follow it

    b.   know my friend realizes I come from the heart even if the advice doesn't solve the problem

    c.   often feel drained, as though I have taken on the weight of my friend's problem

d. try not to get too involved in my friend's personal crisis

e. first help my friend find the truth in the problem and then suggest how he or she might find a just solution

19. I wish I had more control of

a. my temper

b. my heart

c. my worrying

d. my time

e. my fears

20. I do my best work when

a. I am in charge

b. I love what I am doing

c. I know I can be of service to others

d. my environment is uncluttered and I feel centered

e. I am able to approach the project from as many angles as I need to before committing to the final direction

KEY TO ANSWERS FOR THE FIVE ELEMENT PERSONALITY QUIZ

If your answers were mostly the letter

- *a* you are predominately Wood element
- *b* you are predominately Fire element
- *c* you are predominately Earth element
- *d* you are predominately Metal element
- *e* you are predominately Water element

THE FIVE ELEMENT TEST

Each of the following five tables, A, B, C, D, and E, contains twelve words or phrases. Check the words or phrases that most accurately describe your personality, behavior, or traits.

Of course, these words or phrases often describe us all at some time or other. What we are establishing in this test is which ones describe us accurately and consistently in most situations or behaviors.

For instance, in Table A you might check *competitive* because you are willing to stand up and fight for your beliefs or for what is yours. But that does not accurately describe a competitive personality—one who is always competing, is forceful, and above all needs to win. Just as a person who can be romantic with their loved one might not be considered a romantic personality—one who approaches most relationships and situations from a heart-first, above all else, romantic perspective.

TABLE A	TABLE B
competitive	romantic
leader	magnetic
impatient	scattered
warrior/protector	whimsical
focused	animated
challenging/push boundaries	sparkling
big personality/loud	charming
temper	talkative
independent	spontaneous
forceful	performer
be in control	fun/funny
	expressive

TABLE C	TABLE D
stable	perfection
caretaker	cool
child-oriented	precise
worried	logical
nurturing	organized
dependent	analytical
predictable	practical
connected to others	poised
comfy	aloof/reserved
supportive	disciplined
passive	critical/cutting
food-oriented	authoritative

TABLE E

mysterious

wise/wisdom

defender/seeker of truth

academic/intellectual

argumentative

determined

contemplative/dreamy

persuasive

imaginative

cautious

restless

sensual

KEY TO ANSWERS FOR THE FIVE ELEMENT TEST

- Table A represents the Wood element
- Table B represents the Fire element
- Table C represents the Earth element
- Table D represents the Metal element
- Table E represents the Water element

FIVE

Characteristics and Traits of the Five Element Personalities

A FEW PEOPLE FIT NEATLY into stereotypical personality categories. Most of us, however, are a little of this and a little of that. I know some who are "perfectly Wood" or "the quintessential firefly Fire type," but most are a combination of two, sometimes three, of the Five Element personalities.

The following profiles of each of the Five Elements are to help you determine which elemental type, or combination of types, you relate to most.

David, one of my students, recently told the class he couldn't decide which element he was since he identified with every emotion and characteristic. I asked what situations gave him stress, and he immediately replied that his upcoming state medical board examinations were extremely stressful.

"How does that make you feel?" I asked.

"Terrified," he shot back, giving me a look that also said *How else am I supposed to feel?!* I waited a minute, and then he started to smile. "Oh, terrified . . . I guess that makes me Water. But, seriously, isn't everyone terrified?" he asked, turning to the rest of the class, who were also preparing for their boards.

"I'm more worried," said Linda, our class earth mother. "I get in a dither and can't concentrate. That's always been my problem."

"What about you, Robert?" I asked another fourth-year student, an ex–college basketball player.

"Nah, I'm all right. I'll do okay; I'll be mad if I don't do well, but I'm okay with it now," he said with a confident shrug.

David laughed and then asked, "That's all we've got to do to figure out someone's element? Ask them how they respond to stress?"

"That's one big clue," I agreed, studying his face. "We all have many more clues on our faces, but knowing which emotion emerges when you're under stress gives you a head start for when you later begin to learn how to interpret those facial features."

If you feel that none of the dominant emotions especially resonates with you, or if it seems that they all do, ask yourself what gives you stress, and how you feel under stress. You should begin to see a pattern emerging that will help you to identify your Five Element type.

THE FIVE ELEMENT EMOTIONAL TRAITS

The Defining Emotion

We noted that each of the Five Elements has one dominant emotion associated with it: Fire and joy, Earth and worry, Metal and grief, Water and fear, Wood and anger. The emotion that consistently surfaces when you are under stress physically, mentally, or spiritually helps to define your Five Element personality type.

It is not how you deal with this emotion but simply that this is the particular emotion that emerges that is significant. Let's suppose you are predominately a Water type and therefore your core emotion is fear. Does that mean that you are wildly fearful, too scared to take a risk or even step out your door? Not by a long shot. It merely means that when stressful events occur in your life, such as being startled, confronted, encountering unfamiliar situations, or experiencing a significant loss, the primary emotion that you will immediately feel will be fear.

Or not. While it is true that a person who is acutely phobic of many things in life is considered to be an excess Water personality, the complete opposite way of dealing with fear is also true. The person who never experiences fear by denying its presence, or who is constantly pushing the envelope of fear, is also a Water personality type. Again, it's not how people react to the fear, but simply that the fear is consistently their dominant emotion in stressful situations.

Evel Knievel is my favorite model of a Water personality who deals with fear in his own unique way. He has propelled his motorcycles over the tops of burning barrels, barely skimming the flames, jumped his bike over fourteen Greyhound buses, and been towed at two hundred miles per hour behind a race car while holding on to a parachute. His whole life has been dedicated to pushing the boundaries of fear. Evel Knievel's defiance of fear is as much a Water trait as the agoraphobe's response to fear by not leaving home.

It is natural and healthy to feel all of the core emotions at the appropriate times and under the appropriate circumstances. If you never, ever feel anger, that is not healthy. If you deny your grief in a severely sad situation, that is unnatural. Any emotion that is suppressed or denied has as much of an effect on us as our excessive or out-of-control emotions.

Understanding the characteristics, traits, and behaviors of the five different personality types deepens your understanding of yourself and others, enriching your life in a multitude of ways. The more intimately we know our family and friends, the easier it is to observe their reactions and behaviors, helping us to assess which personality type or types they fit. But what about strangers, or the people you do know but who never give you a clue as to what emotions and feelings motivate their behaviors? This is where Mien Shiang is an invaluable tool. Since each face shape and facial feature is associated with one of the Five Elements, you can know a great deal about anyone simply by observing and studying his or her face.

The Gifts and Challenges of the Emotions

Historically, the personality traits of the Five Elements have been presented in negative terms. As you have probably already noticed, the five significant emotions associated with the five basic personality types appear to be rather critical, except one. In the beginning of my workshops someone will inevitably glance at my handouts coupling the emotions and elemental types and exclaim something akin to "The only happy people in the world are the Fire people! I want to be Fire." With joy as the Fire person's primary emotion, the Fire types certainly do seem at first glance to have it far better than everyone else. In response, I explain that something was lost in the translation from the ancient Chinese dialects, and that the joy of the Five Elements more realistically translates to too much joy, or mania. That sufficiently dashes all hope that any of us are here on our life's journey scot-free of adversity, doesn't it?

In a way, that is the point. It is the Taoist belief that we are here, on our life's journey, to learn and to grow. Each of us is born with innate gifts and innate challenges. Our gifts can be a challenge to us at certain points of our lives, and the lessons learned from our challenges often turn out to be our greatest gifts. Suppose you are a Wood personality, and your primary emotion is anger. Most people can see the challenge of anger, but they have difficulty seeing the gift of anger. Yet, when you realize that the appropriate expression of anger is about protection, you can then see how harmful it is to yourself (and to others) not to fully utilize your natural gift. And as you will learn later when we explore the Wood personality in greater depth, the other side of anger is passion. If you suppress one, you will inevitably suppress the other.

To be healthy, happy, loving, evolving, and giving beings, we must discover our true selves. We must embrace and explore our natural abilities so that we may fully realize our potential.

THE QI FOR EACH OF THE FIVE ELEMENT BODY TYPES

In the following personality profiles, when you study the body traits of each, remember that the state and direction of the Qi gives us a quick clue when trying to determine someone's elemental type.

The Qi can also tell us if someone is out of balance physically, mentally, or spiritually. For instance, if you have determined that your friend is predominantly a Wood type, you would expect his healthy Qi to emanate from his feet or legs and to move steadily and straight up his torso. But if his Qi is sluggish or even undetectable, you know he is out of balance. See if you can determine where his Qi is "stuck," and that might give you an idea of where he is cutting off his energy or holding his stress, and what effect that might have on his overall well-being.

Wood	moving steadily upward, coming from the ground as though from the roots of the tree
Fire	moving quickly upward, often frenetically
Earth	emanating from the lower belly or thighs, moving downward to the earth below
Metal	stillness in the chest, as though holding the breath
Water	in the belly, in slow circular or undulating movements

THE WOOD PERSONALITY

emotions: anger/passion; color: green; organ: liver;
sense organ: eyes; expression: shout; shape: rectangle

Anger: The Emotion of Wood

All Wood people have a temper. Not necessarily a quick temper, nor even a frequent one, but a big one. When they do get mad, they get *mad*. My best advice is that when it happens, duck. They like to slam and throw things. This is the Wood person's most serious challenge: how to express their innate anger appropriately and constructively. Rage attracts rage in others, keeping the anger alive and growing, and often dangerous. You don't need to be a psychologist to know that constant, unchecked anger wears you down mentally, emotionally, and spiritually.

Some Wood types overcompensate for their temper by being overly nice, but you can feel their underlying anger and need for control. You can see it, too, in the intensity of their eyes, and in the tension in and around their eyes, jaws, shoulders, and chest.

In my classroom and seminars I always ask if anger is good or bad, and close to 100 percent of the time the consensus is that anger is always bad. When I suggest that anger can be a positive emotion, I am met with adamant arguments (often from repressed Wood types).

Righteous anger, I have to explain, is a positive and integral component to keeping our societal values and behaviors in check. The Wood person who uses his or her anger appropriately is often the person who protects us. It is the self-righteous and abusive anger that has given anger such a bad name. It's important to remember the beneficial uses of anger, and to respect the positive sides of the emotion. When you learn more about the Wood personality's traits and physical appearance, you will see that many law enforcement agents and military personnel are Wood; they are using their gift of righteous anger to protect others.

Passion is the Wood person's complementary emotion to anger. It is as much their gift and challenge as anger is. To live your life passionately, to fully embrace everything that you do and feel, does not guarantee you a perfect life, but it will be a powerful and productive one. The challenge, especially for the Wood person, is not to let your passions overwhelm you so that you become insensitive to other people and situations.

Of course, we all have anger—not just Wood types—and most of us have a hard time suitably expressing it. You will be healthier in mind, body, and spirit if you convey your anger appropriately and in the moment. But that's not always possible. How many times has a supervisor, coworker, or employee infuriated you, but expressing your anger would only have made matters worse? Many similar circumstances require us to hold in our anger. What do we do then?

If we cannot express the anger when it originally comes up, we need to release it as soon as possible. Stored, old anger is toxic and can take its toll on our health. A good first step is to acknowledge that you are angry. This admission can allow you to let the anger fall away. We hold on to our anger for a myriad of reasons, and whatever yours may be, try to see that you can gain much more by letting go than by holding on.

Acupuncture has been found (not only by Traditional Chinese Medicine, but by Western medical studies, too) to be a great release for stored, old anger. Regulated exercise such as walking, bicycling, tai chi, Qi Gong, and yoga helps, too. Competitive exercise is great for blowing off steam, but since it is competitive, it isn't good for releasing anger. You don't have to give it up, but you might want to find a balance and use each type of exercise for different reasons.

I wish I could say that, like anger, we all experience passion. But that's often not true for all of the elements. If passion is not one of your natural gifts, open your heart and mind a little to the idea of living more passionately. See how it feels; think about how it could enhance your relationships or even your work. It might not come easily or quickly, but I truly believe that your life will be improved with even a little bit more passion.

Wood Personality Traits and Characteristics

WOOD PERSONALITY'S KEY CONCERNS

growth	control
focus	domination
drive	enforcement
boundaries/rules	learning patience
competition	learning forgiveness
anger	justice
aggression	understanding others' points of view
power	future (development and growth)

Children grow faster in the springtime,
the season of the Wood element.

Wood people are born leaders, though they don't always have the best leadership skills. Woods don't take orders well, and they don't like to be questioned, so it's hard for them to be team players. Just like the tree with which they are associated in the Five Element theory, they are strongly rooted in their beliefs, especially about their own abilities, ideas, goals, and approaches. So strong are their beliefs in self, it's difficult for them to see situations from different points of view. Wood people are good at enforcing what they want or believe. What makes it slippery is that they are more interested in enforcing what they *believe* to be true, rather than what really *is* true. Once they are committed to an idea, they don't want to be bothered by the facts. As you might imagine, many politicians and corporate heads are Wood.

The more excess-Wood one is, the more one is likely to acquire things of status and value that reflect one's power.

The nature of Wood people is to move forward or up, so if they become stuck or are only moving laterally, they can quickly become depressed. Making plans is important because planning represents the future and movement. If they cannot participate in planning and progression, they will become unduly angry, moody, unfocused, and frustrated.

Wood people are self-referential. To win them to your side, present the issue to them in terms of how it will affect them and their interests.

WOOD RESPONSES TO LIFE-CHANGING EVENTS AND ISSUES

taking control	circumventing
dominating	overplanning or underplanning
intolerance	standing up for the underdog
breaking / pushing the rules	indecision

When life-changing events and issues occur in their lives, Wood people go into action. They are the doers, not the followers. They will quickly try to take control and lead the way to resolution. If they have to circumvent or break a few rules, so be it. But under extreme stress they can either overplan or freeze and become indecisive. Not willing to give up control, they'll become dominating and intolerant of other people's input. They believe so strongly in their own good intentions of restoring justice or rescuing the underdog that they can lose perspective. The more you fight Wood personalities for control, the harder they will hang on. Believe it or not, the best way to get Wood people to listen to you in adverse circumstances is to relax, or even tease them. As long as you don't appear to be challenging them, they will listen to you and stop fighting.

Wood Relationships

Wood people get along well with other Woods as long as they are fighting for the same causes. Fire and Wood are a great combination, especially romantically, since the Fire person is "fueled" by the Wood person's energy, and Wood feels powerful through his or her effect on Fire. Because Wood controls Earth in the Five Element Cycle of Control, that relationship is better for the Wood person than for the Earth person, unless the Earth person is happy serving the needs of the Wood person. The sharp and cutting Metal person can keep the Wood person under control, but can have a difficult relationship with him or her for the same reason. The Water and Wood relationship is a compatible one. The Wood person can help Water to focus and stay on path, while Water feeds the Wood person's energies and helps him or her to reach down to the root of issues and feelings.

Wood and Boundaries

The Wood person definitely has an issue with boundaries. Wood is always creating them and breaking them down. Wood is very aware of what belongs to him, and where his physical and personal boundaries begin and end. He does not have an open-door policy; if he invites you in, you are probably welcome. If you cross a boundary without permission, you will evoke an angry response.

I tell my students that the Wood's unofficial motto is *What is mine is mine, and what is yours is mine*. The obvious downside of this philosophy is that the Wood person will easily invade your space, whether it's your side of the couch, your office space, or your country, because it's his nature. He could be invading as a bully, or because he wants or needs something in your space and trusts his invading motivations to be honorable. That you might object to or question his good intentions will probably anger him—even though the reverse situation, you invading his space with your own good intentions, would not be tolerated. Wood has an explicit double standard about boundaries.

The upside to Wood people pushing boundaries is that they are the protectors of society, constantly looking to right the wrongs of the world. If a loved one, friend, or even a stranger is unjustly treated, it is the Wood person's nature to actively right the wrong, and a Wood will not hesitate to break down any doors or barriers, physically or emotionally, to protect and rescue. Woods are powerful adversaries and defenders.

EXCESS WOOD EMOTIONS AND BEHAVIORS

angry	compulsive
restless	hypersexual
unfulfilled	insomnia
dissatisfied	tense
irritable	

DEFICIENT WOOD EMOTIONS AND BEHAVIORS

lethargic	anxious
depressed	nervous
unassertive	impotent
easily overwhelmed	frigid
hypersensitive to insults	

THE WOOD PERSON'S TRAITS AND CHARACTERISTICS

temper	loud
leader	confident
competitive	protective
passion	assertive
focus	innovative
rooted	self-referential
active	driven

The best medicine for Wood people is to slow down and smell the roses. Meditation is a proven cure for Wood people, but it's hard to get them to sit still long enough to try it.

Creativity, without competitiveness, can heal the stressed Wood person. Focus helps Woods make decisions and accomplish their far-reaching goals. Passion, the wonderful other side of anger, helps Wood people to fulfill their dream of making the world a better place.

The Wood Person's Physical Traits

THE WOOD BODY

The shape associated with Wood is the rectangle, and that is what the Wood body resembles. Think of pro basketball players and their long, strong, rectangular bodies running across the courts. Because Wood people are physically active, they tend to have little body fat. Their arms and legs are tight and sinewy, with defined musculature. If you study Wood people who are standing still (not always such an easy feat, getting them to stay in one place!), you will see that their energy, or Qi, comes from the ground, as though they are rooted, and goes upward, as the sap of a tree flows up to the top. The healthy dispersion of a Wood's Qi is for it to continue up the body and disperse in a focused manner from the eyes.

Unfortunately, though, the Qi often gets trapped in the shoulders and chest, or behind and around the eyes. It is the tension and suppressed anger that cause this stuck Qi. A calm and focused Wood person's Qi will disperse fluidly, and the shoulders, chest, and eye areas will soften and relax.

There are two Wood body types. I have dubbed them the Redwood and the Cypress. Just picture any professional basketball player and you have the quintessential Redwood body type: a tall, strong, lean, tight body that is in constant motion. The second Wood body type is similar, but the Cypresses are shorter and more compact. Think of those magnificent Olympic gymnasts who thrill us with their arduous routines. Every bit as athletic as the Redwoods, the more compact Cypresses use their focus and energy differently, and their bodies reflect the difference. While the Redwood basketball player is in constant motion, aggressively invading or defending his own territory, the Cypress gymnast waits, still and focused, until the whistle blows, then suddenly is a whirl of motion, a force of extraordinary strength and concentration. And then the Cypress lands and is again perfectly still. These are both Wood personalities, and both body types reflect their competitive, focused, and intense natures.

THE WOOD FACE

Just like the Wood body, the Wood face is a long rectangle. It is longer than it is wide, with thick eyebrows, prominent brow bones, focused eyes that often seem to be piercing, especially when they are angry, and a squared jaw. Most Wood people's complexion has tones of green, often called olive. When a green, or brownish green, tone or marking suddenly shows up on the face, especially near the brow bones, eyes, or jaws, we look to see if that person is experiencing excessive or repressed anger.

 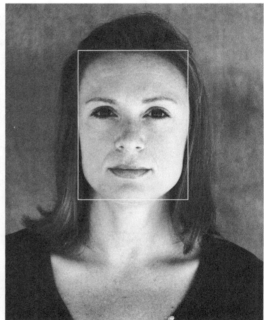

A Wood face

THE FIRE PERSONALITY

emotions: mania/joy; color: red; organ: heart;
sense organ: tongue; expression: laugh; shape: peaked

Joy: The Emotion of Fire

Something was lost in the ancient Taoist translation of joy, the emotion associated with the Fire element. The true meaning is too much joy, an excess that in the present day we would call mania. When Fire people are feeling balanced, they certainly do experience and radiate joy from deep within their hearts. For a Fire person, joy equals love. Without love, there is little chance for joy.

Unfortunately, for Fire, love often does mean romantic love. A Fire person who is not loved and does not love can experience severe depression and withdrawal. Though familial and platonic love is extremely important, too often it just isn't enough. This is heartbreaking not only for Fire people, but for those who care for them. It's hurtful to feel that your love isn't enough, or the right kind.

Despair is the complementary emotion to joy. Sadly, this is the state that Fire people experience far too often if their hearts are not full of or open to love.

Fire Personality Traits and Characteristics

FIRE PERSONALITY'S KEY CONCERNS

love	emotional stability
happiness	relationships
fun	spontaneity
shame	blame
trust	intimacy
bonding	intuition
betrayal	attention
abandonment	

When Fire people are happy and healthy, they sparkle and exude love and joy. Their spontaneity, invariable laughter, delightful whimsy, and extraordinary charm keep them at the center of their vast, eclectic assortment of friends. Fun is the key to their every relationship and venture. If they do not have fun at work, they quit. If learning is not fun, they will fail, no matter how smart or bright they are. If they're no longer having fun with their mate, they get depressed and eventually leave or manipulate their partner into leaving. They frequently have difficulty parenting babies; they do better once the children grow older and they can all have fun together.

Fire people need love like other people need air and water. They also need other people to feel complete; they simply are not good at being alone. If they do not love or feel loved, they tend to feel shame; they are ashamed of not being lovable or of having an empty heart. This often leads to severe depression.

Their need for constant reassurance and approval causes Fire people to bond too quickly or inappropriately, ending in misunderstandings and hurtful situations. This results in their not trusting themselves or anyone else, without realizing how they orchestrated the misunderstandings by rushing or pushing the relationships. This same need to be connected to others makes Fire people excellent performers, glowing from the attention and adoration that comes from loved ones and strangers alike. While they shine in the limelight, they can fall into a dejected slump the moment they're offstage.

They are not only great performers when they're onstage. Fire people are born storytellers; they have creative exaggeration down to an art. Everything is bigger than it really is: They tell tall tales, not lies. And they have the most creative excuses.

When Fire people hear music they have to move. Rhythm is fundamental to them, especially since the heart is the Fire person's associated organ. It makes them feel calm and balanced. Jolting and nonharmonious sounds distress them, however, actually making them irritable and angry.

Though Fire people have quick, bright minds, their energy is scattered. They remind me of fireflies: bright and beautiful, flitting around, hard to catch. The ancient Taoists said that just as fire cannot sustain itself but must be fueled by wood, the Fire person's emotions burn out easily and need to be fueled by others (most often by the Wood person). For Fire people joy comes from without, not from within. As much as they seek love, they also bring great joy to others. The problem is, they often don't recognize the depth or worth of their effect. When Fire people are hurt, they isolate themselves, hurting their hearts even more deeply. It's amazing to see them snap right out of a depression when even nominal friendship and affection is offered. They are exceedingly intuitive with others, but not so much with themselves.

FIRE RESPONSES TO LIFE-CHANGING EVENTS AND ISSUES

loving	overbonding
optimistic	self-isolating
gets to the heart of the matter	inappropriate
self-blaming	vulnerable
entertaining	shame
joking	

When life-changing events and issues occur, Fire people become the center of the event or issue by trying to cheer up others or to protect them from the distress or pain. This can be a great gift, or it can be intrusive. The problem is that the Fire person is not good at distinguishing the gift from the intrusion. Fire people are so sensitive to emotions and pain of the heart that they overidentify and overbond with others to the point of sacrificing their own peace of mind, or even safety, to try to help ease the sorrow and anguish.

Their hearts are in the right place, but they often act inappropriately when attempting to cheer up their friends, or even strangers. Fire people need to be reminded that a good cry is fitting at a funeral—or even at a wedding. It's not their job to keep everyone happy and entertained.

Part of their need to fix the heartaches of others reflects their own insecurities. If Fire people felt more lovable, they could more easily separate themselves from others' unhappiness. A little reassurance, warmth, affection, and love can go a long way to remind the Fire person of his or her worth.

Fire Relationships

Fire people can have lots of fun and loving experiences with other Fire people if they are willing to share the attention. They need to be careful not to start off with fast, intense relationships, which can quickly burn out or erupt in flames.

Fire people love Wood people because Wood fuels Fire's energy and makes them feel lovable. Wood people love Fire people in return because the way the Fire people light up when Wood people are around makes Wood feel powerful. Wood and Fire are good partners in most relationships, especially romantically. Fire and Earth personalities don't have much in common, but the Earth person can be amused by the Fire person, in small doses, and the Fire person often enjoys the calm, settled nature of the Earth personality. Metal and Fire people have an interesting dynamic in that the Fire person's scattered energy can be too distracting for the organized Metal person. Or, sometimes the Fire person's warmth is just perfect to melt the Metal person's cool exterior. If they are in the mood, Metal people are great at organizing the Fire person's eclectic behavior. Water puts out fire, and that's just how Water people deal with flighty Fire people. They can be a good balance, or the Fire person can feel too subdued by the Water personality.

Fire and Boundaries

Boundaries are one of the Fire person's major issues. Their behavior frequently resembles bright, flickering flames that invade and burn up everything in their path. Because Fire people are all about their feelings and emotions and the need to bond, they have little patience for relationships to develop at what would be a comfortable pace for most others. The Fire person is the brand-new employee who thinks it's perfectly appropriate to invite the CEO (whom he hasn't even met yet) for a barbecue the following weekend.

The Fire person is easily and frequently infatuated and will push too quickly for intimacy on all levels. If you meet someone new at your local café one morning and suddenly find she is sharing personal details of her life and then invites you to her birthday party next week, you have probably just met a Fire person who misunderstood your natural friendliness as an overture to forming a deep and instant bond. If you are not as adventurous as Fire people in forming quick friendships, don't be surprised if they don't pick up on your hints to take it slowly. It's unfortunate, but the Fire person may feel rejected, making you feel unnecessarily guilty. Or, he might not notice and flitter away looking for fun around the next corner.

EXCESS FIRE EMOTIONS AND BEHAVIORS

disorganized	flighty
scattered	break commitments
hyper	unclear
confused	immobilizing heartbreak

overreacting	self-blaming
overbonding	self-isolating
too trusting	shame
inconsistency	

DEFICIENT FIRE EMOTIONS AND BEHAVIORS

joyless	unpleasant
loveless	uncaring
practical	unavailable
cold	predictable
independent	

THE FIRE PERSON'S TRAITS AND CHARACTERISTICS

loving	spontaneous
charming	impulsive
animated	scattered
whimsical	intuitive
funny	magnetic
shame	flirtatious

Fire people are at their healthiest, physically, emotionally, mentally, and spiritually, when they take care of their heart emotions. Several scientific studies have proven that loneliness and lack of love and intimacy bring on physical illness. It is especially essential for Fire people to stay connected to others and not isolate themselves when hurt or feeling ashamed. Even the littlest show of love can lift the heart a lot. Pulling in scattered energies and slowing down to pay attention to the reality of the Fire person's life, rather than the romantic wish of what it could be, goes a long way toward healing the Fire heart.

The Fire Person's Physical Traits

THE FIRE BODY

The Fire person has an elongated, slim body: a long waist and narrow hips, with the upper body narrower, longer, slimmer, and weaker than the lower body.

Fires have either a very straight posture, or they slump. Both postures protect the heart. If you hold yourself very straight and tall, your trunk provides an inflexible barrier surrounding your heart. Slumping, with shoulders rounded, also gives the impression that you are protecting your heart from vulnerability and hurt. No matter the posture, most all Fires have weak-looking, underdeveloped, or slightly caved chests.

Fire people are always moving some part of their body, tapping their feet, fidgeting in their chair, swaying to the music. If you want to torture Fire people, tie their hands behind their back and then ask them to tell you a story. You'll see that if their hands are tied, so are their tongues.

Ask Fire people to stand still so that you can sense the direction of their Qi, the energy in their body. Of course Fires will think that sounds like quite a lot of fun and will be eager to stand before you and have you look for their elusive Qi. This will be an amusing venture. You can make a silent bet with yourself before you begin on how many times you will have to remind them to be still. Eventually you will see that their Qi rises upward, but unlike the Wood person's Qi, whose energy travels up steadily and strongly from a strong rooted place in the ground, the Fire person's Qi shoots up from the ground and races up the legs and long torso. The clearer and healthier the Fire person is, the more the Qi will disperse from the chest, the heart area, and their sparkling eyes. When Fires are out of balance, their Qi gets stuck in their chest, overprotecting their hearts.

To me, the Fire body actually looks like a long, slender flame, flickering as though susceptible to any breeze that flutters along.

The Fire face is oval, with a somewhat pointed chin. Fires are known for their bright, open, and sparkling eyes. Rather than specific features being associated with Fire, it's the tips and points of all the facial features that define the Fire traits: the tip of the nose, the bow and ends of the lips, the outer eye corners, the arc of the eyebrows, and the tips of the ears. The more pointed these tips are, and the more they are angled upward, the more they are considered Fire traits.

Dimples are considered Fire charm, freckles represent the scattering of the heart's energy, and a cleft chin is called the performer's chin, a true Fire trait since Fires love attention and entertaining.

Fire people often have a reddish or even flushed complexion. When red tones or markings such as blotches, pimples, or little red veins appear, especially on the tips of any of the features, we consider the possibility that the person has excessive emotions relating to the heart, especially heartache.

A Fire face

THE EARTH PERSONALITY

emotions: worry/sympathy; color: yellow; organ: stomach;
sense organ: mouth; expression: sigh; shape: square

Worry: The Emotion of Earth

Earth people, when learning that their associated emotion is worry, start worrying about it. It is appropriate to worry if your children are late, if your bank account is overdrawn, or if you have just lost your job. But when you ruminate about every choice and decision you have made or turn the possibilities over and over in your head to the point where you can no longer make your decision, your worry is Earth worry.

The trouble with worry is that it seldom goes anywhere, except round and round. Soon the Earth worrier is weighed down with confusion. Confusion goes round and round, too, but it also gains momentum, bringing on anxiety and helplessness. Both worry and confusion are heavy emotions, and Earth people feel buried by their weight. They feel the worry and confusion churn in their stomachs.

The most effective way to get out of the spinning cycle of worry and confusion is to get in touch with your instincts. Grounding yourself can be as simple as keeping both feet on the ground, breathing deeply, and consciously trying to release the physical discomfort that you feel in your stomach. It will clear your head and body so you can feel your instincts instead of the worry and confusion, and move forward.

Children of Earth people complain of being smothered by their parent's over-worry. Adventurous and curious children need the freedom to experience their own lives, but instead the Earth parent teaches them to be practical, not take risks, and play by the rules. Inwardly the child senses that this isn't for his own good, but for the parent's peace of mind. What should be natural and healthy separation between parent and child becomes a full-blown battle for independence. This leads to estrangement, further confusing the parent, who laments and pleads with the child to remember "all that I've sacrificed for you."

Sympathy is the complementary emotion to worry and is healthier and less intrusive. With sympathy, Earth people can extend understanding and compassion without overpowering themselves or those they care for so deeply.

Earth Personality Traits and Characteristics

EARTH PERSONALITY'S KEY CONCERNS

worry	consistency
confusion	comfort
nurturing	pleasure
comforting others	children
support	food
stability	collecting

The ancient Taoists described two types of Earth personalities, who at their core are quite similar, but have quite diverse behaviors. We call them the Soft Earth and the Mountain Earth personalities.

THE SOFT EARTH

Soft Earth people are the caretakers of the world, happiest when they are connected to loved ones, especially their children. Most likely, their family and friends describe them as the quintessential earth mother or earth father. Stability and consistency are a must for them. They want to stay in one place, go to the same shops and cafés, and keep the same friends year after year. They don't like surprises, and spontaneity is not an adventure; they need to know what's going to happen.

Soft Earth people need to be connected to others as much as the Fire people do, but for vastly different reasons. While the Fire person's connection is about love and the heart, the Earth person seeks connection to be needed, to nurture and support others. This connection to others is Earth people's anchor in their world.

They feel abandoned when their loved ones are not physically present; they need to touch to feel connected. If their loved one is talking on the phone, essentially connected to someone else, they will more likely than not give them a little tap on the back or lightly stroke their arm as they walk by.

Soft Earth people are the eternal parents. Often they had immature mothers, so they start young by parenting their own parents. They give such abundant and great advice because they have so much experience taking care of others.

The Earth personality so wants to please; it's not easy for Earth people to accept their own faults, or those of their loved ones. Rather than rectifying mistakes or poor behavior, they make excessive excuses, usually by misplacing the blame. A common statement could go like this: "Oh, Jim blew up again during dinner last night, but it's only because his boss is giving him a hard time; and the kids in Jenny's class are mean to her, that's why she's failing math."

Soft Earth people are accommodating, always doing for others to the point of finding themselves overextended. They are eager to please and can't say no, even when they know they will not be able to keep their promise. They then find themselves in their familiar cycle of worry and confusion.

THE MOUNTAIN EARTH

Mountain Earth personalities have the same issues as their "softer" counterparts, but they are directed and connected more outwardly. Their concept of family extends to community or even the world, and they are less sentimental. They are stable, grounded to the earth, and immovable when they are pursuing their goals, which they do much of the time. They hear the word *stubborn* frequently, but are much too stubborn to let it bother them. Winston Churchill is my favorite example of the Mountain Earth. He even looks like a solid, unmovable mountain. Churchill was known for his earthy needs for pleasure. In nearly every photograph we see of him he has a cigar in hand, and a glass of good whiskey or port is often nearby. Soft Earth personalities will fight to the death to keep their children safe, happy, and frequently at home. Churchill displayed the same needs, but his children were his countrymen, whom he devoted his life to protecting, and also the colonies, which he did not want to let go.

Both Soft and Mountain Earth people love their comfort and pleasures. The Soft Earth might prefer a big, comfy overstuffed chair, while the Mountain Earth enjoys a big, comfy leather chair. They both love their creature comforts, particularly food. There is nothing that food can't cure. The most miserable people on the planet are Earth people on a diet. Do anything, but don't take their food away. Since weight is probably a problem, it's best to talk to them about good nutrition, or eating healthily. Just don't say *diet*; all they hear is the *die* part of the word.

Earth personalities are slow to move and slow to respond. They need time to fully digest information and feelings, the same way they slowly digest their food. It is easier for them to give emotional nourishment than it is for them to receive it. A major source of pain is in expecting that their nurturing and nourishing will be reciprocated without having to ask. They are frequently hurt and often martyred because of this. How do you know when Earth people want a shoulder rub? They walk up and start rubbing your shoulders. Their expectation is that when they are finished, you will reciprocate. When that doesn't happen, they are hurt or angry, but they stuff those feelings. If you ask if anything is wrong, they will sigh and say nothing.

EARTH RESPONSES TO LIFE-CHANGING EVENTS AND ISSUES

taking care of others	overnurturing
supportive	accommodating
expectation	eating
worry	fussing
confusion	freezing

When a major life-changing event or issue occurs, Earth people are most concerned with the emotional aspect. How do they feel? How does everyone else feel? They can sometimes be the take-charge people, but they will always be the take-care people.

If the situation is akin to a natural catastrophe, Soft Earth people are an immensely reassuring influence. They provide nurture and assist those in charge of restoring order and calm. They are terrific supporters when they have a respected and able leader. If they don't trust the leader, they will not budge. It's like trying to move a mountain, even if there is chaos and crisis all around them.

During a major event, the Mountain Earth can be a strong leader, finding one center spot from which to assess the situation and the individual abilities of his team members. From here, he will delegate responsibility. These Earth types are the calm in the storm, grounded and immovable in their decisions and actions.

Earth Relationships

Earth gets along with Earth socially, but not in business or on projects with a deadline. Earths need outside motivation and don't easily find it with each other. Though Wood controls Earth in the Five Element Controlling Cycle, Earth and Wood people usually get along famously. Wood likes to lead and Earth loves to assist a great leader; they can make each other shine. Earth people are so grounded and easygoing that Fire people can seem to them like annoying gnats buzzing around their comfy, quiet world. Conversely, the Fire person likes to bask in the Earth person's calming influence. It's an interesting paradox.

Metal and Earth have a good relationship when Metal people let Earth people nurture them; the Metal person's aloofness is a challenge to the motherly Earth personality. If Metal people can have their own nice and orderly physical space, they don't seem to mind the Earth person's clutter and messiness. Earth and Water people are just too opposite. Water needs to move, and Earth likes stability and familiarity; they have a hard time of it.

Earth and Boundaries

Most of Earth people's problems in relationships are due to their boundary issues. When they care about you, no matter what your relationship, they want to mother you. Too often, though, it feels like "smother." It's as though they want to merge with you, to become one.

A former student calls spending time with her Earth mother-in-law similar to being suffocated by a heavy, wet woolen blanket. "If I try to get a little distance, she gets hurt. She won't tell me, but I can see it in her eyes, and especially around her mouth; she pinches her mouth so tight, it's got to hurt. I'm exhausted for hours after she leaves. And she's starting to respond to our oldest daughter that way when she doesn't want a hug from or to sit next to her Nanna. I can see my daughter's confusion and guilt, but I don't know how to help her."

Earth people have such a true abundance of love and caring that it is heartbreaking when they don't know how to share it appropriately, or how to receive it. Though it might not be your nature to nurture, try it anyway; give the Earth people in your life even a tiny bit of what they give you, and you will have made a wonderful difference.

EXCESS EARTH EMOTIONS AND BEHAVIORS

passive	feels but won't show anger	hunger
martyr	denial	deprivation
others before self	overworry	unreliable
merges with others	nervous	needy
conforming	obsessive	bitter
self-blame	disapproving	refuses to ask for help

unnurturing	inconstant
aloof	unsettled
unstable	uncaring
rigid	

THE EARTH PERSON'S TRAITS AND CHARACTERISTICS

grounded	worry	oversocialized
stable	confusion	accommodating
supportive	connected	overextended
loving	consistent	messy
warm	crave comfort and pleasure	sentimental
comforting	food integral	loyal
slow moving	fear change	no boundaries, especially with children

The Earth Person's Physical Traits

THE EARTH BODY

Earth people do not have hard bodies, no matter how many times they go to the gym. They can be in shape and have great-looking bodies, but they will be soft bodies, even if they are thin. Even an extremely thin Earth person will still have little soft padding on the chest, upper arms, and belly. Earth people are not sinewy; they are soft and round, even their muscles. It's safe to say that Earth people give the best hugs.

Earth personalities are grounded, and so are their bodies. They even have short legs, bringing them closer to the ground. Healthy and balanced Earth Qi emanates from the belly and moves slowly downward to the ground. When there is an imbalance, their Qi feels heavy and gets trapped in the lower belly or thighs. Earth people don't like to be physically active. Sitting in their comfy chairs and eating their comfy food is going to stagnate their Qi and emotions. They need to get moving, physically and emotionally. Even a daily twenty-minute walk is a healthy start. If you care about your Earth friends, get them to take a walk with you a few times a week. They probably won't go on their own, but if they know you need their company, they'll do it for you.

THE EARTH FACE

The Five Element shape for Earth is square, and so is the Earth face. It's a little wider than it is tall (as opposed to the Wood's rectangle face, which is taller than it is wide). Earth people have distinct jawlines; full, generous mouths; and soft pads on their chins, tip of nose, cheeks, and upper eyelids. Their skin is soft and they have creamy complexions.

I tell my students that they'd better like the Earth body and face since most of us have become more Earth in appearance and behavior by the time we reach old age.

Many Earth element people have a yellow or sallow tone to the face. When yellow patches or tones occur on the face, mostly around the mouth and chin, it indicates the Earth emotions of worry and confusion are in turmoil. This is of particular concern in Earth's inability to digest—not just food, but information or the repercussions of an upsetting situation.

 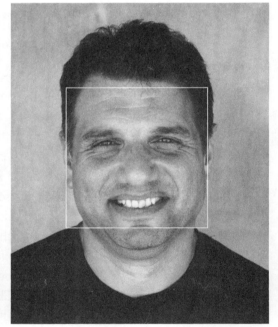

An Earth face

THE METAL PERSONALITY

emotions: grief/compassion; color: white; organ: lungs;
sense organ: nose; expression: weeping; shape: round

Grief: The Emotion of Metal

While everyone experiences grief, Metal personalities' innate challenge is to endure the deep loss they feel in all facets of their being. Metal peoples' challenge is to replenish a loss that they have difficulty defining and comprehending. When pressed, they say they feel incomplete and empty, but they can't articulate why.

Grief has several stages, including shock, numbness, denial, anger, depression, and resolution. The progression culminating in resolution is appropriate to events of great loss. Metal people, however, are often stuck in the first three stages. Then they pull back and overprotect themselves, anesthetizing their feelings. While others might see them as cool, aloof, or even stoic, they are more accurately in shock or denial of their overwhelming sense of loss.

The complementary emotion of grief is compassion. Metal people's deep sense of loss gives them much empathy for the suffering of others.

Metal Personality Traits and Characteristics

METAL PERSONALITY'S KEY CONCERNS

criticism	adequacy
appearance	protection
perfection	letting go
organization	holding on
praise	searching
practicality	understanding
quality	details

Metal people illustrate the prototype of elegance. They are poised, proud, proper, and have impeccable taste. The Metal person can appear to be aloof and so perfect that others can't imagine what they could offer of worth to this prince or princess. It's no wonder Metal people feel lonely so much of the time, and sad that their wonderful strengths are the very traits that keep others away. Insecure and competitive people often misunderstand and feel threatened by the Metal personality. It isn't fair, especially since fairness is one of Metal's primary concerns and attributes.

In Traditional Chinese Medicine, Metal is the element associated with the lungs, and the lungs are all about air—taking it in and letting it out. It's a good metaphor for the Metal personality, who is concerned about air, too. Putting on airs, an air of wealth, the air of being above it all, an air of snobbishness: These are the protections the Metal person uses to keep from getting too close and from being exposed.

Metal people are on a lifelong quest for perfection, and keeping up appearances at least gives the impression of success. Sometimes the illusion is more important than the reality. After all, if you look rich, or if it appears that you are successful, well, then darling, you may associate with those who are, and you shall soon have it all, too. Too often, sensitive Metal people hide their vulnerability behind appearances.

Metals' sense of loss, of something missing from their very core, results in their never feeling "good enough." Metal people are unusually hard on themselves. Everything they do seems inadequate or insufficient, even though everyone else may be singing their praises. They seek praise, yet when they do receive it, they don't believe it. They know they could have done better, or have been better. It's never enough. Their resulting sadness over their inadequacies is kept private. They are mortified if anyone sees them cry or falter; they don't want the attention or the pity. Keeping a stiff upper lip is paramount, but it's hard to maintain. Therefore, Metal people withdraw to protect their feelings and reputation. The quest for perfection is a lonely and impossible path.

Words have an immense effect on Metal people. We have seen that they long for praise, yet when it comes, they cannot hear it. On the other hand, they hear criticism loud and clear. No one is as devastated by criticism as Metal people, and no one can slice as deeply with words as they can. One cool look and a few sharp words from Metal can cut you to the bone.

Naturally, anyone who seeks perfection values quality. The Metal person must have the best. Of everything. Though money is important to Metal people, having "the best" can exceed the monetary value as long as it is avant-garde or cutting-edge. When Metal people get nostalgic, it is for quality: Manners used to be so much better than they are now; they don't make good cars the way they used to; you really can't get good help anymore.

If Metal people cannot have what they want now, they will not accept substitutes; instead, they will suffer through their deprivation.

Because they are not overtly demonstrative and affectionate, Metal people's sincere offerings of concern and kindness are often overlooked. Metal people have a unique sense of selflessness and altruism that enables them to be generous philanthropists. It's interesting that they frequently make their bequests anonymously.

METAL RESPONSES TO LIFE-CHANGING EVENTS AND ISSUES

criticism	practicality
protect	organize
orderly	resignation
needs clarity	cynicism
distance	feels inadequate
withdraw	

Metal people convey authority, and others naturally respond to their cool, calm, collected manner. If they tell you to evacuate the building, you will. When they tell you those stripes look great with the plaid, you'll wear it—and you'll look great. (Okay, not if you're another Metal, but the others will do it, and they will absolutely look great.)

Metal responds to life-changing events and issues with coolness and detachment. Metals assess the situation and find a practical resolution. They are the calm not only before the storm, but during the winds and the devastating aftermath as well. If Metal people had a motto, it would be *A place for everything and everything in its place*. When I tell my corporate seminar groups this, it always elicits good-natured finger-pointing to the Metal people on the team. Not only do their immaculate desks and offices look as if they were torn from the pages of designer magazines, but so do their work presentations, and even their well-put-together selves. There's not even a paper clip, design, nor hair out of place.

This is a person you want in charge in a crisis. The downside is that Metal people are like this in their personal lives, nearly all the time. They need to be encouraged to view life, and to experience it, in a less exact and practical manner. Perfection may be a lifesaver in an emergency, but it can be severely life-hampering in everyday existence.

If others are not involved, and the life-hampering situation affects only the Metal person, he is in danger of resigning himself to his fate. We have all been puzzled by a competent, capable, and sharp-witted person who does not stand up and fight for his own self, but instead seems to coolly and acerbically stand aside and watch "fate" take its devastating toll. This is probably a Metal person who does not feel cool or particularly witty, but his pride will not let him expose his vulnerability. He would rather take the loss than experience the humiliation of being so "common."

Metal Relationships

Metal people often prefer being with their own kind. They have the same work ethic and the same reserved approach to personal relationships. Metal gets along better with Wood than the reverse. The Metal personality can either sharply cut the Wood person's energy or finely whittle it to reshape the Wood person into presenting a less challenging or confrontational behavior. This can be a good team, or it can infuriate the Wood person when he realizes he is not in control. Fire people are great at melting Metal people's icy rigidity, and Metal's cool, collected manner calmly organizes Fire's scattered energies. Earth and Metal relationships are better in small doses or at a distance. Metal people are dismayed by Earth people's messiness and lack of orderly thinking, but they do like their warmth and nurturing, in little measures and without the touching and hugging. The Metal personality admires the Water's creativity and investigative meanderings, but has trouble with the Water's dreaminess and (what appears to the Metal person to be) lack of focus. Water people respect the Metals' clarity but feel inhibited by their lack of spontaneity.

Metal and Boundaries

Metal people love boundaries. After all, their motto is *A place for everything and everything in its place*. This does not apply only to their things, but to their emotions, behavior, and expression of their feelings as well. A Metal person is an ardent enthusiast of proper and appropriate conduct, with rules to ensure this conduct stays within boundaries. Infractions are dealt with promptly, usually by cutting off the relationship with the offender.

The one constant that severely violates Metal people's boundaries is criticism. Disapproving words poke away at their fragile emotional borders, making them hypersensitive to any constructive feedback or dialogue. A Metal child who had critical parents will become a harsh self-critic and overachiever who can never do well enough.

EXCESS METAL EMOTIONS AND BEHAVIORS

overly critical	intolerant
cold	overorganized
harsh	overly protective
cutting	cynical
biting	sarcastic
acerbic	resigned
false pride	contemptuous
haughty	rigid

DEFICIENT METAL EMOTIONS AND BEHAVIORS

unclear	too accepting
cannot receive	meekness
too trustful	scattered
undiscerning	

THE METAL PERSON'S TRAITS AND CHARACTERISTICS

cool	sharp-tongued
elegant	mentally proper
poised	reserved
appearance-oriented	witty
control	impeccable
analytical	enamored with the past
defined	captivated by the future
principled	cutting-edge
precise	cutting off
need boundaries	practical
sharp-looking	self-reliant

The Metal Person's Physical Traits

THE METAL BODY

Metal people's bodies are tight yet delicate-looking, as though they might snap in a strong wind. Not all Metal people are thin, but they don't often have any "extra" fat or fatty pouches, either. If they are carrying extra weight, they still have small wrists and ankles, and their chests often appear to be frail, with the skin stretched tightly over their noticeable collarbones. Overall they do not appear to be strong, and usually they aren't.

Metal people have beautiful postures, and this has as much to do with their Qi as with their natural elegance and poise. Every other of the Five Element personalities has Qi that flows in a pattern or direction that is recognizable to the practiced observer. However, the Metal person's Qi is barely perceptible. It doesn't flow, but flutters lightly in the chest. Often, Metal people look as though they are holding their breath, but the ancient Taoists say that they are using their breath to protect their fragile Qi.

THE METAL FACE

Metal people are often exceptionally attractive. Most top male and female models have the perfect Metal face: angular, sharp features and flawless, tight skin stretched across their long, elegant, thin noses and high cheekbones.

High eyebrows are a Metal trademark, giving the appearance of aloofness. While the Metal people do enjoy their privacy, it's more their shyness that keeps others at bay.

The complexion of most Metal element people is less notable for its color than for the sheen to the skin. The Metal person's skin seems to glow. This is less shiny than a luster or polished look.

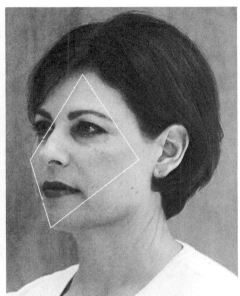

A Metal face

THE WATER PERSONALITY

emotions: fear/wisdom; colors: black/blue; organ: kidneys;
sense organ: ears; expression: groan; shape: amorphous

Fear: The Emotion of Water

About five years ago a good friend and I were strolling through Union Square in San Francisco on a busy Saturday. A self-styled motivational speaker had rigged up a tinny amplifier and was shouting into his microphone, "If you have fear, you are weak. You will fail!"

I groaned and rolled my eyes at my friend, a doctor of Traditional Chinese Medicine and a gifted teacher of Taoism. Maybe because it was the weekend and he was feeling spirited, my friend rushed up next to the park orator and shouted into his microphone, "If you have fear, you have the gift of wisdom! May we all be so blessed!"

I heartily agree with my friend's Taoist understanding of fear and fervently reject the other view. Unfortunately, his opinion is not a popular one in our culture.

As with all our emotions, fear can immobilize us if we succumb to it. If we meet it head-on, it can be a great teacher. After all, we are all socialized by fear. You do not instruct tiny toddlers to avoid a burning flame by explaining the physics of fire, nor keep them from running into the path of a moving car by explaining velocity, speed, weight, and matter. You do teach them to be safe by instilling a little healthy fear in them; it's all their little minds can grasp at that age. I have never met a mother who has not uttered the words "Careful, you'll burn yourself!" or "Don't run into the street, you'll get run over!"

We continue to socialize ourselves with fear when we wonder about the consequences of our actions. It's the what-ifs that make us wise and safe: What if I run with scissors? What if I let my friend drive when she's been drinking? What if I let my dogs bark and I ignore my neighbors' complaints? The rational person has a healthy fear of doing the wrong thing. It's normal to fear stabbing yourself with scissors if you are careless, to fear that your friend will hurt herself or others if she is impaired, and to fear being a selfish and unkind neighbor (who might just get sued).

As we mentioned earlier in regard to Evel Knievel, many Water types are so afraid of being controlled by their fear that they go to extremes to control it. All of us have fear, not just the Water types. However it affects you, look for the gift and the lessons. Push your boundaries of fear wisely. Be brave enough to take some risks, and smart enough to be a little scared when it's appropriate. It's finding the balance that will enrich your life.

Water Personality Traits and Characteristics

WATER PERSONALITY'S KEY CONCERNS

fear	reassurance
trust	security
determination	decisiveness
safety	knowledge
loyalty	truth
restlessness	courage
time	commitments
patience	

Water people's determination is inspiring. They are like a flowing river intent on reaching the ocean. Sometimes they push forward with the energy of rushing rapids, other times they are happy to meander like a lazy stream, taking all sorts of side trips. No matter how many tributaries they explore on the way, boulders they have to go around, or dams they have to break, Water people keep steadfastly heading toward their destination.

If you are in a hurry, Water people will test your patience. Most often they are late because they are dreamy and highly imaginative, spending lots of time in their heads and not enough on schedules.

There is something alluring and mysterious about Water people. They even look mystical, deep, and wise. These naturally sensual people are not unaware of their power of seduction, they just pretend to be. A former neighbor of mine, Allessandra, was a Water type. She was the most seductive person I've ever met, yet she wasn't overtly sexual. She had a mysterious promise in her large eyes and behind every word, whether she was asking for a favor or arguing a political point.

Water people are wonderfully creative and exceptionally imaginative. Most Water people I know had imaginary friends when they were children.

With fear as Water people's associated emotion, it is not surprising they have difficulty with trust. Water people are forever challenging loyalty and intent, and they will question you about everything, well beyond normal curiosity. It's no wonder they are such good litigating attorneys.

The Water person is a seeker of truth, especially spiritual truth. Many Water people travel the world in this quest and may experiment with many religions and spiritual practices. Their predilection for wanting to see justice meted out can also cause them to overreact in their search for truth. They have to tame their inner zealot.

The sense of dread Water people carry with them is palpable, even when life is good. A Water type can suddenly be panicked by what others might see as a minor event. Water people can use their bravado to hide their great need to be reassured and consoled, missing the comforting that they crave.

WATER RESPONSES TO LIFE-CHANGING EVENTS AND ISSUES

fear	reassuring or consoling others
safety assessment	determination
risk assessment	bravery
taking risks	courage

| maintaining or establishing stability | panic |
| questioning | paralysis |

Water people are best in major event situations when there isn't a threat to life and safety. When they feel they are in physical danger, they can freeze like the proverbial deer in headlights. They are the people who need to be pulled from the sinking boat or pushed out of the way of the speeding car. Their panic causes them to go into debilitating shock physically, emotionally, and mentally.

When the life-changing event or issue is not overtly threatening to life and limb, Water people can be quite brave and courageous, taking calculated risks others wouldn't even consider. They need to be careful not to overassess issues of safety and risk to the point of being too late to make a difference. Water people have a calming effect because they are so reassuring. They gain strength and mastery over their own fears when they encourage and console others.

Water Relationships

Water types work well with other Water people on creative projects, with both of them willing to meander and try all sorts of imaginative possibilities. They tend to lack patience for intimate relationships with other Water people, given the other's dreamy lack of focus—especially if the focus is taken away from them.

Water and Wood relationships are good. The Water person helps the Wood to see a broader view, and the Wood keeps the Water person focused.

Water and Fire people have inconsistent relationships. If the Fire person is too scattered, the calm Water person can bring tranquillity. That will work sometimes, but more often the Fire feels too inhibited. On the other hand, if the Water person is too dreamy, the Fire person can get that Water boiling and moving forward.

Earth and Water people have trouble. Mix them together and their energies turn to mud. Earth people like to stay in one place, enjoying their creature comforts, and Water people are curious, wanting to move, explore, and be adventurous. You just can't budge an Earth person who doesn't want to move, and you can't tame the restless flow of the Water person.

Metal and Water people have good relationships. Water's sensuality warms the

Metal's protective reserve, and Metal helps direct Water's creativity and imagination. They complete what the other lacks, and there is seldom any competitiveness.

Water and Boundaries

Water people are forever pushing boundaries, but not as overtly as the other elemental types. Water people quietly seep through the cracks, softly meander into your space, or seduce their way into your private thoughts before you realize they are there. If you turn them away, their determination will bring them back, as quietly and subtly as before.

When Water people are more blatant in breaking down boundaries, it's with their great verbal skills. They can, and love to, make an argument for anything just for an opportunity for debate. They will win this debate whether or not they believe in the position they have argued.

Water people carefully protect their own boundaries. They use their natural fear to assess the weak spots in their walls and keep them in good repair. The sense of mystery they create about their boundaries just adds to their sensual appeal. It can take a while to realize that a Water person has delicately and skillfully pushed you out of the way because she has just created another new border that you cannot cross. Water people do enjoy a little ambiguity.

EXCESS WATER EMOTIONS AND BEHAVIORS

panic	indomitable
anxiety	impatient
dread	restless
dismay	inconsolable
confusion	

DEFICIENT WATER EMOTIONS AND BEHAVIORS

fearless	questioning self
wavering	disloyal
unsure	cannot recognize truth
reckless	indecisive

determined	mysterious	spiritual
restless	persuasive	just
risk-taking	argumentative	inquisitive
imaginative	wise	apprehensive

The Water Person's Physical Traits

THE WATER BODY

The Water body is sensual. Even if thin, the Water person has shape, a body that curves and seems to sway with motion. Water women have what is sometimes called an hourglass figure.

It's not always easy to tell exactly what Water people's bodies look like because they like to drape themselves in loose, flowing clothing, creating an alluring mystery.

Water people's Qi is centered in the stomach and moves languidly in a small circle, or sometimes the movement is undulating, like a gentle wave.

THE WATER FACE

Water people have big, open eyes that go from startled and aware when they are uncomfortable, to dreamy and soft when they are relaxed. The ancient Taoists said that Water people seduce with their eyes first and their minds second.

The most remarkable trait on a Water person's face is the gentle fullness in the lower cheeks. They have strong, determined jaws, and wide, often prominent foreheads.

Many Water element people have blue tones in their faces, especially under the eyes and often near their hairlines and jaws. When there are sudden blue markings on the face, it's usually because the person is having difficulty expressing or acknowledging her fear.

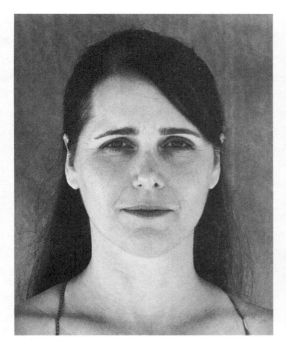 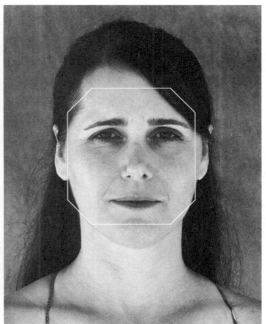

A Water face

part two

HOW WE READ FACES

SIX

What Do We Read on the Face?

WE HAVE ESTABLISHED THE HISTORY of Mien Shiang, its roots in Taoism, and how Yin and Yang and the Five Elements will help us to interpret our findings. We know why we want to learn to read faces. It's time to find out how to read our faces.

Now is the time to spend hours in front of the mirror. Start staring at your family, friends, and strangers in ways that will probably make them uncomfortable—until you master the art of subtlety. I always advise my students to develop that skill quickly, though I confess that I enjoy hearing the stories of some of the more outrageous miscommunications that have occurred due to overenthusiastic applications of newly learned Mien Shiang skills.

In learning how to read a face, we first need to know exactly what it is we are looking at and looking for when we examine our faces. Most people rightly assume that Mien Shiang is a study of the facial features, but we study more than just features. We are also looking at the size and shape of our faces. We study the different, subtle, and changing skin colors that appear and disappear. We analyze the sizes, shapes, and po-

When we read the face, we look at the

shape of the face

size of the face

colors of the face

shape, size, and placement of each feature

markings, moles, shadings, lines, and wrinkles

sitions of each of our features: ears, hairline, forehead, brow bones, eyebrows, eyes, cheeks, cheekbones, nose, mouth, chin, and jaws, and all of the lines, shadings, markings, bumps, and indentations that appear on or near each feature.

EACH FEATURE'S OWN IDENTIFIABLE CHARACTERISTICS

We get precise information from each of our facial features since each feature is associated with specific emotional or behavioral characteristics. As soon as you learn the characteristics associated with each of the twelve features, you have a huge new wealth of information about yourself and everyone you know.

INTERPRETING THE FEATURES' CHARACTERISTICS

More is more and less is less in Mien Shiang. The larger the ear, the more risk-taking ability one has by nature. The more prominent the brow bones, the more controlling the nature; the narrower the jaw, the less determination.

CHARACTERISTICS OF THE TWELVE MAJOR FACIAL FEATURES

Ears	risk-taking ability, longevity
Hairline	socialization
Forehead	parental influence
Brow bones	control
Eyebrows	passion, temper, pride
Eyes	receptivity
Cheeks	confidence
Cheekbones	authority
Nose	ego, power, drive, leadership
Lips/mouth	personality, sexuality
Chin	character, will
Jaws	determination

These, of course, are generalities, but generalities are a good place to start with Mien Shiang. In Part III, as you continue to study each feature in depth, you will see that it is a much more complex art and science. For now, though, these guidelines will get you used to analyzing faces and learning a bit about your own and other people's natural gifts and challenges.

It's time to take another long look in the mirror and see which feature jumps out at you. An interesting exercise is to ask a few people who see you frequently to identify which feature of your face captures their instant attention. You might be surprised how varied the answers will be, especially if they do not focus on the same features of your face that you do.

Start looking at your family, friends, and coworkers, and see if those with prominent jaws are indeed the most determined, or if those with high, defined cheekbones do have a strong sense of authority.

Of course, as we have learned, we do not read just one feature of the face and have a complete analysis. Each feature and its traits are all part of the big picture, or puzzle pieces that fit together to make the whole. Yet many people do have one or two features that stand out more than the others. This immediately tells us something significant about that person's personality or well-being. Think of Jay Leno and his famous chin, or Angelina Jolie, who is known for her full, voluptuous mouth. Do the personality traits associated with those features match the personalities of these famous faces?

FACE SHAPES

Your bone structure helps determine the shape of your face. So do the soft tissues, muscles, fatty pouches, and skin that cover these bones. Our bones don't change once we reach adulthood, but the other components are in slow but constant flux. As we age, gravity pulls our features downward. Weight gain can round out one's face, and weight loss can make it look longer. Even our emotions can affect the shape of our face. When we are down in the dumps, that's usually the direction our lower face takes. When we're feeling up, our face actually appears to lift.

While the individual facial features give us the most thorough and varied analysis of a person, the face shapes help add a structure to the whole reading. Few people have a definite face shape; most of us are a combination of two or even three shapes.

Two different face shape evaluations are used by Taoist practitioners of Mien Shiang. One evaluation correlates five particular shapes with each of the Five Elements. These shapes correspond to the personality traits we have already studied in the Five Element personality profiles in Part I. The other evaluation is a more general interpretation, known as the Eight Common Face Shapes. Four of these shapes are the same as four of the Five Element shapes, yet they have slightly different personality traits.

THE EIGHT COMMON FACE SHAPES

The Eight Common Face Shapes have specific features associated with the face shape; it's a more precise "package" than the Five Element face shapes. You won't always see such exact face shapes and features, but when you do, you'll be intrigued at how accurate the personality traits fit those faces.

 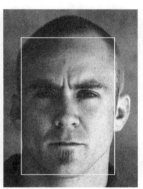

Rectangle: long, strong forehead; flat ears; weak cheekbones; well-defined mouth; strong chin
Personality Traits: intelligent, active, hard worker, self-control, aggressive, introspective
Element: Wood

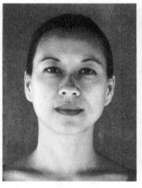 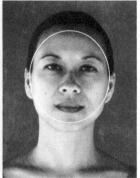

Round: round, strong bone structure; flat cheekbones and cheeks; flat ears; wide nose
Personality Traits: self-confident, mentally sharp, adaptable, sincere, influential, reliable
Elements: Earth, Metal

Square: wide forehead and jaws; strong bone structure
Personality Traits: stable, honest, generous, stamina, strong constitution, decision maker, resists authority, strong willed, physically strong, honorable
Elements: Wood, Earth

Oval: oval, medium nose; flat ears; round cheeks and cheekbones; small or medium mouth; pointed or oval chin
Personality Traits: intelligent, altruistic, diplomatic, charming, perceptive, good social skills, romantic
Element: Fire

 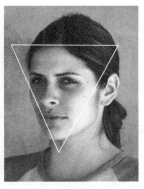

Triangle: wide forehead; prominent cheekbones; normal or thin lips; pointed or oval chin
Personality Traits: strong mental acuity, ambitious, realistic, idiosyncratic, reticent
Element: Metal

Diamond: prominent cheekbones wider than forehead and jaws; flat ears; regular nose; thin or medium mouth; pointed or oval chin
Personality Traits: strong authority, confidence, unpredictable, charming, perfectionist
Elements: Metal, Fire

 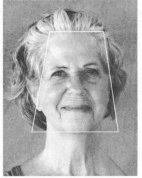

Top Wide Trapezoid: wide forehead; narrow, square chin; full mouth
Personality Traits: creative, astute, inventor, performer, outgoing, inventive ideas
Elements: Water, Wood

Lower Wide Trapezoid: narrow forehead; wide jaw; wide nose; small or medium mouth
Personality Traits: grounded, intuitive, strong willed, good instincts, physically strong, competitive, in charge
Elements: Earth, Water

SEVEN

Inherited and Acquired Facial Traits

*Certain facial traits are inherited from our parents
and our ancestors, while others are acquired
from our own life experiences.*

WHEN SOME PEOPLE FIRST LEARN about Mien Shiang they dismiss it as a parlor trick because they cannot understand how we can interpret individual personality traits. Since all features have been inherited from one's family and ancestors, they might say, how can this be a serious study? I understand their initial confusion, and I do agree that we all inherit features and behaviors, but none of us are clones. (In fact, even clones have their own personalities and behaviors!) One of the most significant scientific/psychological debates of the last many years is nature versus nurture, and I will not attempt to put forth the arguments of either or both sides here. I will describe, however, how the ancient Taoists explained the inherited versus experiential traits in each human being.

OUR INHERITED FACIAL TRAITS

Most of us resemble at least one parent, grandparent, aunt, uncle, or cousin. Though siblings often have no outright resemblance to each other, each one usually has a close likeness to another person in the extended family. My sister, Nancy, and I look nothing alike, yet I look like our father and she looks like our mother. The sons of actor Martin Sheen, Charlie Sheen and Emilio Estevez, don't closely resemble each other, but Emilio is a dead ringer for his father. My friend Alan is a perfect mix of both his parents: He has his mother's smile and his father's nose. Yet, he looks like neither of them. He has a unique look that is quite his own.

We inherit many traits from our ancestors, whom I like to call our ancestral tribes. Scandinavians have distinct facial characteristics: high, broad foreheads, long noses, luminescent, fair skin, and narrow lips. In other words, they have features that have adapted to a cold, dry, harsh climate. A long, thin nose, for example, limits the amount of cold air breathed in, then warms (and keeps moist) the inhaled air on its way to the lungs. Those born nearer the equator have shorter, broader noses; they don't need to warm up the already mild and humid air upon inhalation. And since damp air travels slower than arid air, the shorter the nose, the quicker the air reaches the lungs.

Here we can see the traits that this daughter inherited from her mother: a broad forehead, wide-set almond eyes, a wide mouth, full cheeks, and a long, rounded chin. The features unique from her mother are the downward-curved eyebrows, narrow jaw, and smaller turned-up nose.

So, purely by observing the inherited cultural and ancestral traits and features of one another, we can make general determinations. Still, we must remember that while many traits and features are similar, each person has a distinct look within each cultural and ethnic group. Each feature can be larger or smaller, wider or narrower, higher or lower, lighter or darker, more luminescent or duller, and shallower or deeper than others of the same heritage.

Veronique is a student of mine. A superb and well-known photographer, she has studied with me for more than five years, both at the university and privately. She is fascinated with reading and analyzing the face and uses it in all aspects of her life and work. During her first semester of studying Mien Shiang, she told the class of an interesting experience she had had while in England the previous year. She had photographed identical twin sisters who had been separated at birth and adopted by two different families. One sister remained and grew up in the London area, while the other sister was raised in Argentina. When Veronique met the sisters, they had recently found each other and reunited after thirty-four years of separation. Had Veronique not been told they were sisters, she would never have known. They looked nothing alike, let alone like identical twins.

All their features were dissimilar, especially their mouths. The sister who had lived in London her whole life had a thin, tight mouth; there was hardly any flesh at all to her lips. Yet, her sister who grew up in Argentina had a full, voluptuous mouth. How could that be, Veronique wondered, when they are identical twins?

Since Veronique and the class had already learned the traits and characteristics associated with each of the facial features, I turned the question back to her. How could thirty-four-year-old identical twins have completely different features?

Veronique thought a bit, then her face lit up. "The food! The English food made that sister swallow her lips!" she said, like the true Frenchwoman that she is.

When we all stopped laughing, I urged her to consider what else it might be. (I would never argue food with the French!) "It must be their experiences," she finally acknowledged. "They had different experiences which shaped their personalities. And the mouth tells us about personality."

She was, of course, correct.

OUR ACQUIRED FACIAL MARKINGS

Our faces accurately record our
chronological passages of life.

As we age, our faces change. We get wrinkles and lines, dark spots and shadings. Though we tend to resent them, these signs of experience are actually good because they are recording our chronological passages of life. They are visual proof that we felt the emotions of our experiences, struggled through our difficult times, and learned the lessons of life. We can rail against them, or we can celebrate them as marks of wisdom that come with age. Remember, people don't value wisdom if they don't value aging. Wear your lines of wisdom proudly and confidently.

Most markings appear on an area of the face that represents the age that the emotional experience first occurred. For the marking to occur, one must feel the experience. If people deny or suppress their emotions when their traumas occur, they will have a notably unlined face in their later years. While they may think they look better, they may not feel better if they haven't experienced the joys and pains that come with living a full life. Last year I gave a workshop at a beautiful Southwestern estate and met Helen, a lovely woman in her sixties. Helen was proud of having no lines on her forehead. I am always concerned when I see people of mature years who do not have lines of wisdom on their face. I can't help but wonder if they have learned the lessons of their life experiences.

Helen was a successful and recognized sculptor, happily married, with healthy grown children and darling grandchildren. However, she confided in me that deep in her being she felt profoundly sad and lost.

"What sad loss did you experience in your teenage years for which you were not allowed to grieve?" I asked.

I could see she was taken aback by my question. When she got her bearings back, Helen revealed that her mother had passed away suddenly when Helen was a teenager.

"And who didn't let you grieve?" I asked gently.

Again Helen looked surprised that I knew this. She told me her story, of how her grandmother, who was a survivor of Auschwitz, demanded that Helen "be strong" and not "indulge" her grief. She was never allowed to cry or express her sadness. In fact, she wasn't even allowed to feel her sadness. While her grandmother had had to sublimate the grief of losing her family during her own teenage years in order to survive, her granddaughter was more harmed than helped by her well-intentioned advice.

"And that is why I don't have lines on my forehead?" Helen asked, more than a little confused.

"I believe so. In Mien Shiang our forehead represents our teenage years, and the lines, scars, moles, and color splotches that appear there represent the upsets of those years. That is why most people have several lines and forehead markings—the hormonal teenage years are rife with trauma and drama. Whenever I see such an unmarked forehead as yours, Helen, I do not assume that there were no teenage upsets, but that there were suppressed emotions from some very big traumas."

We don't develop marks on our faces if we don't feel the feelings connected to our losses and grief. To mark, we have to feel. Our lines, wrinkles, and markings are the visible proof that we have felt our feelings and then moved on. I encourage everyone, including Helen, to be proud and wear their lines and wrinkles as badges of courage and strength.

"You know, I always thought my unlined forehead was an inherited gift," Helen said. "My grandmother had the smoothest forehead for all her ninety years, even though she had a hard life. She was such a stoic. But I always felt she was sad and lonely deep inside."

"I think you did inherit your smooth forehead from her," I said, "but more likely because she passed on to you the same behavior of not feeling your feelings that she had had to adopt to survive her own teenage years.

"Each of you had to face the consequences of not being allowed to feel your feelings when they first occurred."

"What consequences?"

"The profound sense of loss and sadness that has persisted in your life, no matter how good things have been. If we don't learn our lessons when the experiences first occur, we often sentence ourselves to repeating the same painful incidences over and over again. Even if we don't repeat the behavior, the unresolved grief stays inside, eating away at our happiness and peace of mind.

"I can only urge you, Helen, as painful as it may sound, to finally feel those old feelings of loss and grief for your mother. Feel them, experience them, and then let them go. I promise you, it will be the best thing you can do to feel the happiness and love you deserve in your beautiful life."

ACQUIRED FACIAL MARKINGS

Most markings appear on an area of the face that represents the age that the emotional experience first occurred.

For the marking to occur, one must feel the experience.

When marking does occur, we look at each marking, or line, to determine placement, size, shape, depth, color, and shading.

Two weeks prior to this writing, I received a heartfelt letter from Helen. She went to a Hopi reservation shortly after our meeting and spent the next several weeks working with a shaman of the tribe, who helped her to feel and then release her grief. I am thrilled for her newfound happiness and look forward to hearing many more joyous reports from her.

Even though Helen and her grandmother had similar behavioral responses to loss and grief, it is important to remember that no two people experience anything, especially deep emotional feelings, in exactly the same way. Not even if they are raised in the same family and are each present for every family change and challenge. Every single person responds to every single event and emotion in a unique way. To use again the example of identical twins, remember that though they are born as mirror images of each other, they come into the world already distinct from each other: They each have their own identifiable emotions, spirit, and even fingerprints. Whether it was due to their physical position in the womb, or how each reacted to the mother's sniffly nose, or to her indigestion, or to an emotional trauma that may have occurred during the pregnancy, each twin will have a complete and individual response to each event. Those individual responses will likely be reflected in tiny, microscopic differences on the newborns' faces. Those variations can be hard to spot right away, but they are there, just like the twins' subtly different fingerprints.

Everyone is shaped by their life experience:
physically, emotionally, spiritually.

EIGHT

How to Interpret the Gifts and Challenges of the Traits

IT'S PROBABLY NOW BECOMING APPARENT to you that your own face reflects both your inherited and your acquired traits. Some of those traits are gifts, some of them are challenges.

If you have inherited your father's ears—large, smooth, well-developed ears and lobes—then you have also inherited his strong risk-taking ability and his gift of longevity.

Suppose your brother inherited your mother's ears: small and narrow, with short, flat lobes. He has inherited her challenges regarding risk-taking and longevity.

Does that mean that you will live an exciting and long life, while your dear brother will be timid and die early?

Of course not.

It means that it is your basic nature to take risks. You don't need to scrutinize each of the pros and cons of a challenge, you just go for it. The thrill of the risk is exciting to you. You won't always be a winner, but you will be in the arena more than most others, better able to deal with the defeats as well as the successes.

Your gift of longevity means you have been granted a little boost toward making it through the hard times of adversity, illness, and trauma. You will be able to get away with less sleep, more stress, and a richer diet than your brother. It's not a free ticket, though. Many people with beautiful large ears and nice plump earlobes have died young by abusing their gifts. So don't jump off a cliff with a homemade parachute, bet the family fortune at the roulette wheel, or eat and drink whatever you want and expect to live forever. You have a gift that is to be nurtured and protected, not taken for granted or squandered.

Your brother's basic nature is to be more cautious and to consider the consequences before taking a risk. His risks might actually result in more successes since they are well thought out, but he probably won't take as many risks as you. His challenge is to take the leap, and to trust his instincts and skills.

Since he doesn't have the inherited gift of longevity, he will have to work a bit more than you do at being healthy. A good diet, an exercise program, and balanced emotions will all help him achieve a long, healthy life.

USING YOUR GIFTS AND CHALLENGES

As essential as it is to nurture and protect your gifts, it's equally important to use them.

It might seem the easiest thing in the world to make the most of such gifts as confidence, determination, will, power, leadership, and passion. Unfortunately, many people never allow themselves to use these great gifts because their insecurities, childhood restrictions, traumas, or fears are stronger than their gifts.

Children are frequently not permitted to be their true selves. Their family, community, or culture might have strict rules as to how one should behave. This severely hampers the child's natural being and evolution.

A youngster who has nice thick eyebrows is going to have the natural gifts and challenges associated with temper. But if that child is never allowed to express anger, he will never learn the appropriate uses of this essential and healthy emotion.

Not using your gifts may have deep emotional, spiritual, and physical repercussions. This is a good opportunity for you to identify your innate strengths. Doing so will help you to make the most of your precious gifts and to appreciate the lessons to be learned from your challenges.

NINE

The Specific Age Areas of the Face

WHEN WE DESCRIBED ACQUIRED FACIAL markings, we mentioned that they tend to appear on the corresponding age-related areas of the face. These markings record the chronological evolution of our life experiences.

The following 100 Age Area charts show how the age areas proceed chronologically, starting on the ears for ages one through fourteen, then beginning at the top of the forehead at age fifteen and moving across and all the way down the face to the chin to age seventy-five. Ages seventy-six through one hundred continue under the jawline, making a full circle around the head, just behind the hairline, ending with age one hundred under the tip of the chin.

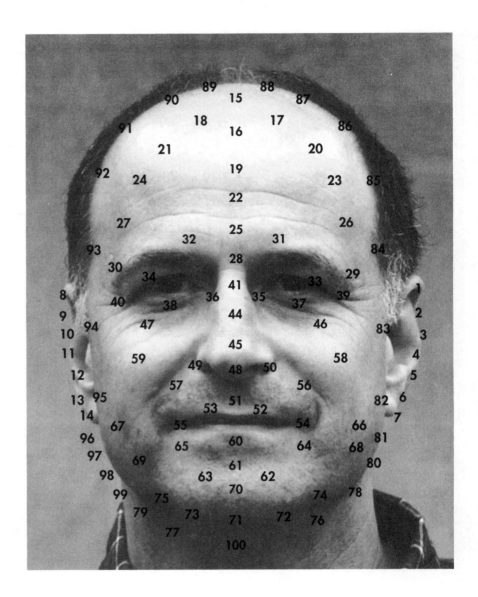

Take another long look in your mirror and find one or two markings, such as a bump, line, mole, protrusion, indentation, or unusual coloration. Then refer to the charts and see if those markings correspond to an age in your life when you experienced disharmony or a significant change in your everyday life. When I was first learning Mien Shiang, I called my sister in Vermont and asked her to check the top of

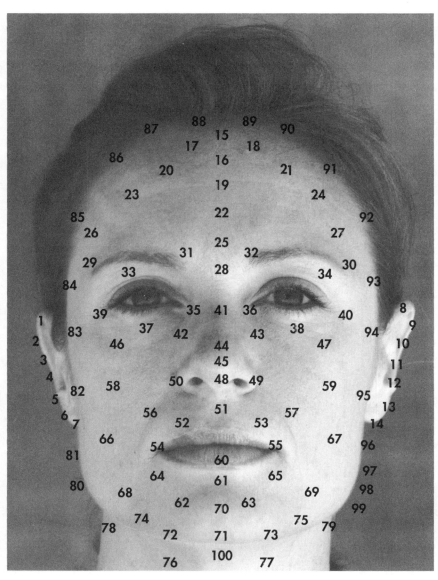

The one hundred age areas for women

my mother's left ear. Sure enough, there was a small white bump at the eight-year-old area. We had heard many times the story of how my mother nearly drowned when she was eight years old, and how terrified of the water she still was all these years later. Now we saw the evidence of that trauma on her ear.

GENDER AND THE AGE AREAS OF THE FACE

Note that The 100 Age Areas charts depict the specific age areas for men, and that the opposite side of the face is true for women. When Mien Shiang was introduced three thousand years ago, men and women lived radically different lives from each other. Gender determined everything, including personal power, career, and acceptable ways to express emotions—or, more often, how not to express emotions. Now, the disparity between the sexes has considerably lessened in many countries. When young girls and boys are treated more and more alike, they tend to reflect their facial markings in the same areas. When I'm doing a face reading, I always ask if the person was brought up in a traditional or modern family and community. I use this information to decide which side of the face might signify the male or female sides.

THE EARLY-AGE MARKINGS ON THE EARS

The following depictions of ages one to fourteen represented on the helix of the ears are the traditional interpretation for men and for women. As in the facial markings, I determine the type of family and community in which a woman was raised. If hers was a traditional upbringing, I read ages one to seven on her right ear, and ages eight to fourteen on her left. If she was raised in a more progressive family and community as described above, I will follow the men's charting.

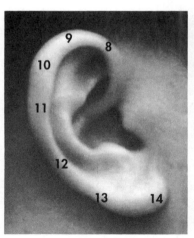
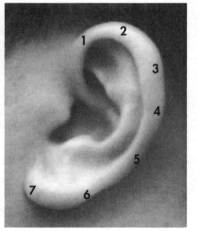

Ages for males one to fourteen years represented on the helix of the ears

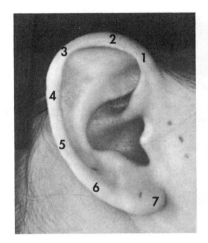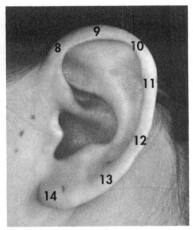

Ages for females one to fourteen years represented on the helix of the ears

There is no exact ruler measurement between the age markings since there are as many different sizes and shapes of ears as there are people. What is sufficient to note is that something noteworthy happened at an approximate age rather than an exact age.

The Two Sides of the Face

THE TWO SIDES OF YOUR face each reveal something unique. The left side of your face represents your true, inner, private self, and your father's influence. The right side represents your outer, public personality, and your mother's influence.

Three thousand years ago it was easier for the Taoist monks to declare which side of the face each parent influenced. Now we have ever-changing family structures and dynamics. Even in more traditional-appearing families, many women assume what used to be considered the father's role, and many fathers are either stay-at-home dads enacting the stereotypical mother role or are more nurturing than their partner. Often an older brother, sister, teacher, or other relative or friend takes up one of the parental roles. What is important to learn from reading the markings and features on each side of your face is not so much the exact person who influenced a dynamic event in your life, but what role that person played during that period and how you reacted to them as well as to the event.

UNMATCHING SIDES

Not all faces are symmetrical. In fact, most aren't. Eyes can be of different sizes and shapes, a nose can bend toward one side, cheekbones can be higher on one side, and mouths can be thinner or lower at either end. Other than models and actors, most clients I work with have never noticed their asymmetrical features until they have their face read. At first some are slightly distressed, but then they are quickly fascinated by what the different shapes and sizes mean. Whenever people have an opportunity to learn more about themselves, they feel more complete and more in charge of their lives.

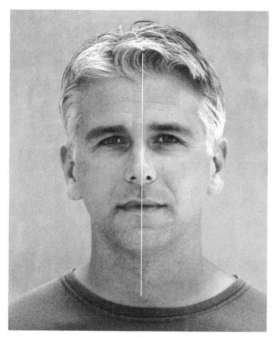

The two sides of the face correspond with the principle of Yin and Yang: The right side represents the outer, public self and the mother's influence; the left side represents the inner, private self and the father's influence

Suppose you meet someone whose mouth is higher on the right than the left. Since the right side of the face represents our outer, or public, face—the face we want to show to the world—we can surmise that this is someone who "puts on a good face" to the outer world. It doesn't necessarily mean that the person is suffering terribly on the inside, but rather that this may be a private person, not prone to wearing his heart on his sleeve. Of course, if you notice other signs of sadness or withdrawal on his face, he could very well be experiencing deep inner unhappiness. As always, we can never make a complete determination by just one feature or marking. It's only one piece of many pieces of the puzzle.

Start looking at people and see which features of theirs aren't symmetrical. It might be more apparent with the features that come in pairs, such as the ears, eyes, eyebrows, brow bones, cheeks, and cheekbones.

Let's say that you have a friend whose left cheekbone is more prominent; it's higher and more pronounced than the right cheekbone. You have already learned that each facial feature has its own identifiable personality or behavioral trait, and that the trait associated with the cheekbones is authority. Based on this information you could most likely determine that your friend feels a sense of inner authority, but has trouble acting on that authority. You might even have felt some frustration in your relationship with your friend in that you have assumed him to be capable and influential, but have been disappointed when he refuses to take control of situations with the authority you expect him to naturally possess.

Though we can read the strengths and weaknesses of specific traits on each side of our faces, we don't always know the reason why someone may or may not have a particular gift or why they do or do not use these gifts.

Knowing that each side of the face represents either the mother or father figure's influence can help you to understand the possible origins. Use your friend with the more prominent left cheekbone as an example. It's probable that his father figure played a strong role in promoting or supporting your friend's sense of authority in his childhood. Or, that his mother suppressed his innate authority, causing him to hide it from the outer world.

If you have a close relationship with your friend, you might want to ask him how he feels about his sense of authority and how he uses it. Don't be surprised to find that his answer matches your Mien Shiang deduction.

A former student of mine has a right ear that is notably larger than his left ear. As I came to know him, I learned what I had first suspected to be true. He is a great risk-taker in all things physical and financial. He skis and snowboards down the most treacherous peaks, kayaks in white water, and loves motorcycle racing. By the time he was thirty-four he had already started, and lost, several businesses. He considers anything and everything in his public life a challenge to be met. I'd never known him, however, to take an emotional risk. If it wasn't a sure shot, he pulled back. When he lost the woman of his dreams because he couldn't make a commitment, he finally decided to work on developing his emotional risk-taking. Doing that, he also came to terms with his father's belief that "real men don't give in to their feelings." I wouldn't say he has become warm and fuzzy, but he does make an honest attempt to recognize his feelings. He tries to feel as deeply as he can at this point. As interesting as he was when we first met, he is now an even more delightfully complex person.

DETERMINING THE YIN AND YANG SIDES OF THE FACE

Ancient Chinese culture demanded that one never show one's true feelings. To save face, to have face, to show face—all meant that you were skilled at hiding your true feelings behind your face. It was essential to project the face of the person you wanted people to believe you were, not who you truly were.

In those days, your public personality was reserved and quiet, while your private life was active and complex. Since being reserved and quiet are Yin qualities, the right (outer) side of the face was the Yin side. And as the qualities of Yang are active and complex, so then the left (inner) side of the face was the Yang side.

In our modern cultures we express our feelings and thoughts much more openly and frequently. Some of us share emotions with dramatic flare, while others are still intent on keeping all their feelings hidden, practicing what the ancients called Thick Black Theory. Overall, we now consider it healthy to be able to express our emotions appropriately, and to be suitably discreet when a situation warrants it. We do not have one circumscribed, national, or unicultural way of behaving and expressing feelings. We are a wonderfully mixed collection of exceptional individuals, many of whom have rich inner and outer lives, and some who have equally sedate inner and outer lives.

No longer can we make a blanket statement as to which side of the face is Yin or Yang. It depends on the person and how he or she expresses true inner feelings.

Look closely at both sides of your face in a mirror. Is one eye larger or brighter? Does one nostril seem narrower than the other? Do both corners of your mouth go up? Is one eyebrow shorter?

Then look to see which side of your face seems to have more energy and vitality. It is easier if you cover one side with a blank piece of paper and study the uncovered side. Then do the same with the opposite side of your face. You will most likely be surprised at how different each side is, not just in size, shape, and proportion of the features, but in the overall energy that we call Qi, or our life's essence.

The side of your face that has more vital Qi is your Yang side, and the other side is your Yin side.

Some faces have vibrant amounts of radiating Qi, and others have more subtle Qi. Don't be discouraged if you don't see the energy right away. It takes awareness and study. I promise, though, that with practice you will get it—you'll see the energy in your face, and in all of your body as well. You will then be able to distinguish which side of your face is Yang and which side of your face is Yin.

As you get used to looking at others in this way, you will soon be able to recognize whether their inner or outer personas are more Yin or Yang.

Some Exceptions

It seems that some people have never had a private thought or feeling. They regale us with every detail of every emotion, usually at high volume and in crowded places. These drama queens and kings like or need to work out their issues in public, and thereby their inner life is marked on their right side.

Another exception is people who suffer from bipolar disorder. Often they have two conspicuously different sides to their face, with more pronounced differences than the normal Yin and Yang energies. Or, depending on the phase of their illness, both sides of the face may reflect either all Yin or all Yang energies.

part three

READING THE INDIVIDUAL FEATURES

ELEVEN

Analyzing Each Feature for Specific Traits

WHAT WE HAVE LEARNED SO far are the broader strokes of Mien Shiang. We are now familiar with certain overviews applied to Yin and Yang, the Five Elements, face sizes and shapes, the two sides of the face, and the general characteristics applied to the features.

This section is an in-depth study where we analyze more closely the traits associated with the *specific* shapes, sizes, angles, colorations, and markings of each facial feature.

Though we look in the mirror at least once every day, most people could not tell you if their own ears, let alone their friends' and loved ones' ears, are positioned high, low, or "in the middle," or if they have one eye slightly smaller than the other, or if their nose bends a bit to one side. Yet these small differences are marks of distinction that speak volumes about one's character, personality, and health, whether in the past, the present, or the future.

We have learned that the facial features are intricately associated with the Five Elements, and that each of the Five Elements is in turn associated with a particular emotion, color, shape, and organ. As we broadened our study, we also learned that each facial feature represents certain behavioral characteristics such as risk taking, anger, confidence, and so on.

As we do our comprehensive analysis of each feature, we will be especially aware of the characteristic, emotion, element, organ, and color associated with each feature.

WU XING CHART
CHARACTERISTIC / EMOTION / ELEMENT / ORGAN / COLOR

FEATURE	CHARACTERISTIC(S)	EMOTION	ELEMENT	ORGAN	COLOR
ears	risk taking, longevity	fear	Water	kidney	black/blue
hairline	socialization	fear	Water	kidney	black/blue
forehead	parental influence	fear	Water	kidney	black/blue
brow bones	control	anger	Wood	liver	green
eyebrows	passion, temper, pride	anger	Wood	liver	green
eyes	intelligence	anger	Wood	liver	green
cheeks	confidence	grief	Metal	lungs	white
cheekbones	authority	grief	Metal	lungs	white
nose	ego, power, drive	grief	Metal	lungs	white
eyes/Shen	receptivity	joy	Fire	heart	red
nose tip	heart emotions	joy	Fire	heart	red
tips of all features	heart emotions	joy	Fire	heart	red
lips/mouth	personality	worry	Earth	stomach	yellow
chin	character, will	worry	Earth	stomach	yellow
jaws	determination	fear	Water	kidney	black

Once you have completed this section of the book and have analyzed all of your facial features, you will conclude which ones represent your strengths and which ones help you to understand your life's challenges.

If, for example, your predominant features are of the Water element (ears, hairline, forehead, jaws), then you are principally a Water element type. If you also have pointed features, which are Fire characteristics, especially your chin tip and nose tip, and the corners of your eyes and mouth, you are a combination of Water element type and Fire element type.

Most of us are a combination of two elemental types (sometimes even three, but that is not as common), though every once in a while we see a face that has dominant features of only one of the elements. I see many professional basketball players who have the quintessential Wood face, with all of their energy in their brow bones, eyebrows, and intense eyes; and a lot of earth mothers do seem to have predominantly Earth features of full mouths and chins and soft, fleshy noses and cheeks.

Many performers, especially the wild and "out there" ones, have completely Fire faces—points on all of the features and lively, sparkling eyes.

I've seen many airline pilots and flight attendants who have classic angled Metal faces with high cheekbones, long, thin noses, and high eyebrows, which accentuate their cool, calm, and collected natures. Just whom you want taking care of business while you're thousands of feet in the air.

When I've taught corporate workshops for design teams, I've often seen quite a few attendees with predominantly Water faces whose outstanding features are their high domed foreheads, determined jaws, and noticeable ears.

When you have determined which elemental type or types you are, compare the results of your personality quizzes from Part I and see if the traits and characteristics represented by your features correspond to the dominant emotions and personality traits from those tests.

DETERMINING THE SIZE OF THE FEATURES

Every once in a while one of my students will have difficulty understanding what I mean by small, medium, or large features. Standard sizes have actually been developed for most features (for example, large ears are classified as more than 65 mm [2.6"] long and 36 mm [1.42"] wide), but that is not practical in the everyday use of Mien Shiang. I imagine most people would be a bit taken aback if their health-care giver suddenly whipped out a tape measure and began measuring their ears, noses, and chins.

Determining feature size is easy. First, ascertain if the feature "fits" the size of the head, and if it is in proportion to all of the other features.

What if you have large ears on a large head? Is it still considered "large" from a Mien Shiang point of view? Absolutely, though large ears on a small head appear to be even larger because of the imbalance of sizes. But, either way, they are both large ears. As you become used to looking at all the features analytically, it will become quickly apparent if they are small, average, or large, and whether they are in proportion to each other. It's simply common sense and practice.

EARS

risk taking/longevity   *fear*   *Water*   *kidney*   *black/blue*
1 through 14

We are used to thinking of our ears as sense organs for hearing and equilibrium, and a great place to hang some pretty jewelry. Or, as my Uncle Sol used to say, their main purpose is to prevent you from going blind since they hold up your hat and keep your eyeglasses in place.

While all of this may be true, the ears also tell us many important things regarding our inherited abilities, including longevity and if we are risk-takers, and they record the major events of our childhood.

Our ears are governed by the Water element, so if you have nice, big, strong ears, we can tell right away that you have some good strong Water energy and personality characteristics. If your ears are tiny and weak, then we can rightly assume that you are deficient in the element of Water in some ways. Of course, we need to check the other Water element features of the hairline, forehead, and jaw before we determine your entire Water element gifts or challenges. But as we have said before, more is more: The more prominent Water features you have, the more likely you are a Water element type of body, mind, and spirit.

ALWAYS CONSIDER THE **WATER ELEMENT** ASSOCIATIONS FOR THE **EARS**

characteristics	risk taking, longevity
emotion	fear
element	Water
organ	kidney
color	black/blue
ages	1–14

A lot more is going on in the reading of the ears than with most of the other features. Besides representing the first fourteen years of our lives and our risk-taking abilities, they also indicate what we came into the world with: our inherited traits, especially kidney Jing; our basic constitution; the base physical health of our sexuality and fertility; and for women, the innate health of the reproductive system.

WE READ THE EAR TO DETERMINE TRAITS AND STATUS REGARDING:

inherited kidney Jing

risk-taking abilities

basic constitution

sexuality related to basic health

fertility

female reproductive system (inner ear)

Kidney Jing

A basic concept in Taoism and Traditional Chinese Medicine is Jing, which is the essence of life. Jing is stored in the kidneys and determines our:

- energy
- strength
- basic constitution at birth
- growth cycles: conception, puberty, menopause, aging
- brain function: how we think, how we execute intelligence

The Tao teaches that we are each born with a certain amount of Jing, and if we use it wisely we will have a long and healthy life. If we deplete our Jing by living too large—too much food, drink, work, stress, play—it is gone forever and cannot be replenished. We can, however, conserve and nurture our remaining Jing by practicing a moderate and healthy lifestyle. Qi- and Jing-enhancing exercises such as tai chi and Qi Gong are especially beneficial.

Good, healthy-looking ears tell us we have good Jing, and good Jing naturally augments our sexuality and fertility.

Those born with large ears are born with a gift of abundant Jing. It can be a

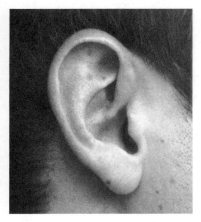

An ideal healthy ear

double-edged sword, though, since big-eared people are often risk-takers, and risk taking can quickly deplete Jing.

A well-defined, large, even, and smooth ear with good color is considered the **ideal ear** because it indicates good health, healthy risk-taking abilities, and minimal inherited or experiential trauma of mind, body, and spirit. A large ear is defined as of generous height and breadth. As we have said before, in Mien Shiang bigger is generally better.

Please keep in mind when we speak about the ideal of each feature that we are not referring to ideal physical beauty, but rather to a healthy physical, emotional, mental, and spiritual balance.

Some Native Americans believe those with well-developed ears can hear the voices of the spirits.

Ear Size

small	cautious, self-critical, introverted, ambitious, thoughtful, well-behaved children
average	normal behavior and reaction regarding fear and risks
large	risk-taker, leader, sociable, sensual, intrusive
different sizes	many challenges, crises, much success in later years

In ancient Rome, people with big ears and fleshy lobes were considered balanced people with generous natures. Those who had small ears with pale lobes were regarded as dangerous in some way.

People with **small ears** tend to be cautious, sometimes to the point of becoming fearful of taking a chance on anything that isn't a sure thing. Their desire for perfection makes them overly self-critical and contemplative, which impedes their naturally ambitious nature. They are wary in most relationships and find it difficult to commu-

WOOD

What makes a person a Wood element?
Members of this group are passionate people and natural leaders. You recognize them by their intense gaze, strong brow bones, prominent eyebrows, and a rectangular face.

◄ *Quintessential Wood*

Quintessential Fire ►

What makes a person a Fire element?
These charming and spontaneous people come from the heart. You recognize them by their oval-shaped face, sparkling eyes, and brilliant smile.

FIRE

What makes a person an Earth element?

Earth people are grounded, supportive people known for their nurturing ways. You recognize them by their full mouths and full, fleshy chins, cheeks, and earlobes.

Quintessential Earth

What makes a person a Metal element?

Cool, clear, and elegant describes these organized and often philanthropic people. You recognize them by their long slender noses, high eyebrows, and prominent cheekbones.

Quintessential Metal

What makes a person a Water element?

Water people are wise and determined seekers of truth. You recognize them by their open, often dreamy eyes; their full lower cheeks; rounded upper forehead; and determined jaws.

Quintessential Water

EARTH

METAL

  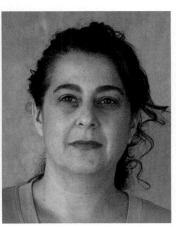

WATER

Wood with Fire: The Wood with Fire person fights for those who have no voice with his passion and charm. His Wood is in his brow bones and his Fire shines in his eyes.

Wood with Earth: The Wood with Earth person can lead others to success while nurturing their talents. His Wood shows in his square jaws and Earth is in his strong chin.

Wood with Metal: The Wood with Metal person has the focus to create a cutting-edge strategy. Her Wood is in her rectangle-shaped face and her Metal in her high, upper cheekbones.

Wood with Water: The Wood with Water person will fight for his dreams. His Wood is in his strong eyebrows and the Water is in his large ears.

Fire with Earth: The Fire with Earth person brings fun to everything with a rock-solid stability. Her Fire is in her sparkling eyes and her Earth in her strong chin.

Fire with Metal: The Fire with Metal person's creativity and perfectionism ensures priceless creations. Her Fire is in the points in her lips and her angled cheekbones show her Metal.

Fire with Water: The Fire with Water person makes friends from the heart, motivating them through her search for truth. Her Fire is in her pointed chin and her Water in her high forehead.

Fire with Wood: The Fire with Wood person is spontaneous, yet still in charge. His Fire is in his oval face and his Wood in his brow bones.

Earth with Metal: The Earth with Metal person can make anything happen with support and poise. Her Earth is in her full mouth and her Metal shows in her prominent cheeks.

Earth with Water: The Earth with Water person brings a grounded perspective and restless curiosity. Her Earth is in her wide chin and her Water in her full lower cheeks.

Earth with Wood: The Earth with Wood person is unmovable when he knows he is right and uses his passion to forge ahead. His Earth is in his broad, strong chin, and his Wood is in his prominent brow bones.

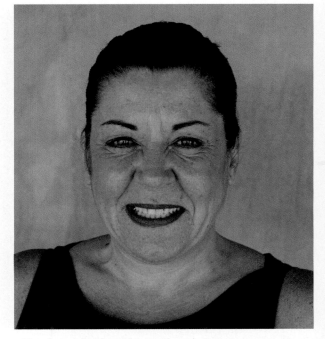

Earth with Fire: The Earth with Fire person's strong will is perfectly balanced by her love of fun. Her Earth is in her full mouth and her Fire in her lively eyes.

Metal with Water: The Metal with Water person balances an analytical mind with a creative imagination. Her Metal is in the sheen that comes off her face, and her Water is in her high, round forehead.

Metal with Wood: The Metal with Wood person tackles a problem with practicality and fights to enforce his opinion. His Metal is in his long, narrow nose and his Wood in his heavy eyebrows.

Metal with Fire: The Metal with Fire person will perfectly organize a project making sure everyone is happy. Her Metal is in her high, angled cheekbones and her Fire is in her dimples.

Metal with Earth: The Metal with Earth person reaches out with compassion and keeps those relationships solid. Her Metal shows in her high eyebrows and her full mouth reflects her Earth.

Water with Wood: The Water with Wood person uses wisdom and passion to lead others to challenge the rules. His Water is in his prominent, rounded forehead and his Wood in his strong brow bones.

Water with Fire: The Water with Fire person's creative imagination and spontaneity makes him a natural performer. His Water is in his strong jaws and his Fire shines through his eyes.

Water with Earth: The Water with Earth person needs unwavering trust, and then she nurtures a project and people to a satisfying end. The Water is in her full lower cheeks and the Earth in her wide chin.

Water with Metal: The Water with Metal person's creative determination is helped by a precise, organized mind. Her Water is in her full lower cheeks, and her Metal in her high cheekbones.

nicate unless they are in control emotionally. Once they do establish a relationship, however, it lasts a long time. In work and social situations they need recognition or they become depressed or defeated.

Those with **large ears** (more than 65 mm long and 36 mm wide) are natural leaders, straightforward and responsible. They are often successful in business, and their outgoing and sensual ways make them desirable social partners. Even though they are big risk-takers, they are not always winners. Gamblers have the same chance of failing as of winning. Whatever the outcome, they're usually ready to jump back into another risky venture. Though often great fun to be around, their extroverted nature can just as often make them intrusive and overwhelming.

I've often wondered about the practice of clipping show dogs' ears. Since the dogs are bred for show and need to be exceptionally obedient, does the ear-clipping make them less risk-taking and more docile?

Some people have decidedly **different size** ears. In general they can expect to struggle more than others might in obtaining success, probably due to having more than their fair share of unexpected crises in their youth. If your ears are noticeably different in size, don't be discouraged. You can achieve your dreams with desire and determination, and you have advance awareness that you will be challenged along the way. It's quite beneficial

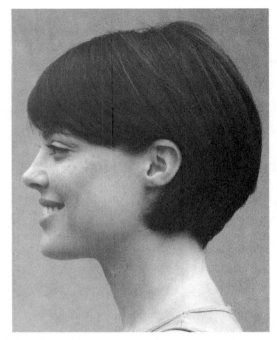

A small ear

Large ears

Ears of different sizes

to have warning of your natural challenges in life, and to be prepared to use your natural gifts to help you get through some of these crises. In fact, many people with different-size ears have great success later in life.

You might also note which ear is larger and concentrate on either your inner personal strength if it's your left ear, or if your right ear is the larger, to nurture your natural strength of coping more easily with the outside pressures of life.

My good friend's right ear is smaller than his left, and he certainly had a turbulent childhood. When he was seven, his father died suddenly and tragically, leaving a devastating void. Soon after, his mother remarried and his young life was laden with emotional and verbal abuse from his stepfather. My friend has an uncanny physical and emotional resemblance to his father. They were both professional athletes with bigger-than-life personalities and many admirers. And both were born with the gift of risk taking and nice big ears. I think my friend's right ear is smaller because he felt unsupported and unprotected by his mother from his stepfather's angry, racist tirades. He suppressed his outward risk-taking behavior at home in order to appear less like his natural father to his resentful stepfather, thereby keeping peace in a chaotic household.

Now that my friend has reached his midthirties, he has forgiven his mother for not having had the courage to stand up for him in his youth. I think their reconciliation has played a significant part in his comfort with being suddenly poised on the edge of great success in his career. I have no doubt that he will continue to succeed and break all sorts of barriers in his creative and competitive field. And I believe that his challenges are what have helped him develop his strong character and determination to live the life he was meant to live.

A student recently showed me a picture of her father when he was twenty-five years old and then a more recent one taken when he was nearly sixty. "Look how much bigger his ears are now," she said with amazement. "How could that happen?"

"First of all, cartilage is one of the few body tissues that continues to grow after we have reached adulthood," I explained. "Sometimes the ears can grow as much as a quarter inch from ages thirty to seventy, though it doesn't always happen. I wonder if something happened to your father after the age of twenty-five that encouraged him to become more of a risk-taker?"

"Most definitely," she said. "My father's family was very wealthy and prominent in Iran, but they lost everything and had to flee the country not long after that picture was taken. They came to Los Angeles with nothing and no one. Because he was the only one who spoke English and he had a college degree, my father suddenly went from being a spoiled young guy who never had to work to the head of the household. In less than a year he scraped together enough money to buy a run-down industrial lot outside of Los Angeles that he turned around and sold for a good profit. He kept taking more risks with properties no one else wanted, and in just three years he could afford to buy his parents a beautiful home in Pasadena.

"He always says that taking those big risks almost did him in. I can't wait to tell him that taking all those risks made his ears grow, which then gave him the ability to take even bigger risks!" she said, laughing.

Caesar was suspicious of thin people and objected to having people with small ears around him.
Napoléon barred a captain from his bodyguard unit because he had "ears as tiny as his mind and pale as his fidelity."

Ear Shape

round ears	outgoing, fun, imaginative, dependable
square ears	sharp, astute, dynamic
long ears	good fortune, intelligent, wise, principled
pointed/faun's ears	astute, likes intrigue, secrets, sensitive
wide conch ears	a gift for music, seeks harmony
protruding inner ear	creative, eccentric, storyteller

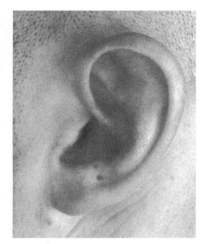
A round ear

Some ears look like perfect semicircles. If your ear is **round,** then you probably have to make excuses to stay home alone every once in a while. Who wouldn't want your company: fun, outgoing, upbeat, inspiring, dependable, and sweetly seductive?

Square ears, squared on the tops, lobes, and sides, belong to sharp-minded, astute people who can easily lead others with their dynamic drive and insight. They can have several projects going at once; in fact, they love to have as many distractions as possible so they don't get bored and lose interest in any one thing.

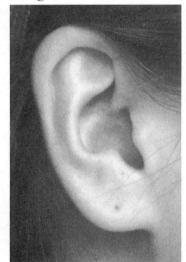
A square ear

Years ago when I first lived in Arizona, I knew an elderly man who with his **long ears** looked like a wise old basset hound. He was a great fan of local theater and the arts, and I would frequently see him at openings and cafés. Though somewhat aloof, he never lacked for company and generously bestowed advice on nearly anyone on nearly any subject, especially on issues of morality and behavior. His standards were high for himself and others, yet he seldom seemed preachy. Since his teenage years his friends had called him Midas, as it seemed that all he touched turned to gold. He claimed to never really understand this since he wasn't particularly ambitious; but for some reason good fortune had followed him from his youth to old age. Shortly after I started my study of Mien Shiang I understood fully: He simply had the gift of long ears!

My students call pointed, **faunlike ears** Mr. Spock ears. I don't know the personality traits of these ears on Mr. Spock's planet, but on ours, they belong to sharp-minded people who just can't help but create a little intrigue and ad-

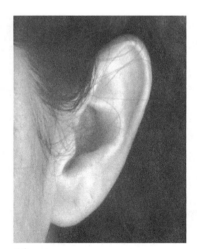
A long ear

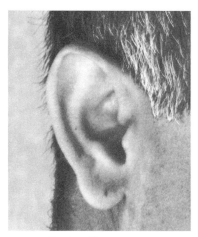

A pointed or faunlike ear

venture wherever they go. I know a man with these ears who has had a series of secret romances, creating great airs of mystery and excitement, even at the risk of people thinking he is having an affair when he's not. Though he is bright, fun, and a great conversationalist, I am sometimes surprised to find that he is more sensitive than he likes to let on, and he uses his charm and laughter to protect his feelings.

People who have a gift for music tend to have "the musical ear," a wide ear opening that resembles a **conch** shell. The old Taoist monks told us that these people are seekers of harmony, especially in relationships.

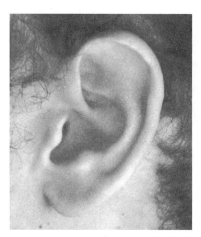

An average ear conch

I've found that the reason they are seeking harmony is because they have an innate sense of drama, stirring up the very disharmony that inevitably throws them un-comfortably off-balance. Their life often resembles an exhilarating piece of music that builds and builds, then turns and ends with a calming note.

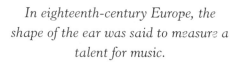

In eighteenth-century Europe, the shape of the ear was said to measure a talent for music.

If the conch ear is the musician's ear, then the **pro-truding inner ear** could be called the fiction writer's ear. A woman I know with this shape of ear is a Holly-wood screenwriter married to a serious-minded college professor who makes sociopolitical documentaries. They nearly divorced after she convinced him to let her codirect one of his films. She is a brilliantly creative, ec-centric, spirited storyteller who kept urging the docu-mentary subjects of their film to "not be so boring! The plain truth is just so—plain! Let's fix that up!" After

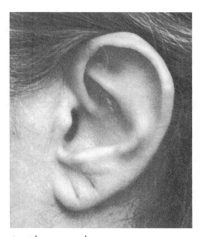

A wide ear conch

much frenzy, her husband ended up making the film alone, and she continues to entertain us on the big screen and at dinner parties with her wonderfully exaggerated stretches of truth, which are just perfect for the fictional tale.

We have two ears and one mouth so we may listen
more and talk the less.
EPICTETUS

The Three Sections of the Ear: Reading for Risk Taking

The ear is divided into three equal sections to determine particular risk-taking abilities, and the broader the section, the more the ability. Large and small ears alike can be broader or narrower in any one of the sections.

The top third of the ear represents financial and mental risk taking, the middle is emotional and physical, and the lobes represent longevity and wealth, which means more specifically the ability to plan for the future.

The three sections of the ear relate to risk taking

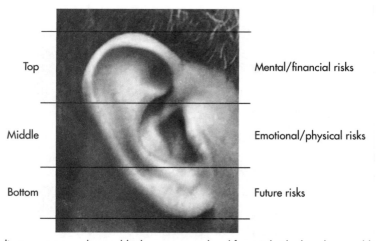

Top — Mental/financial risks

Middle — Emotional/physical risks

Bottom — Future risks

This photo indicates a person who would take more mental and financial risks than they would emotional and physical risks. The lobe seems to be average, so we would assume the person takes average precautions when planning for the future.

Set of Ears

average-set ears	most common, therefore denotes "average" behaviors and insights
high-set ears	realistic, common sense, doesn't like the limelight, steady worker
low-set ears	idealistic, intelligent, affable, action-oriented, likes to have lots of people in life
right ear higher	severed or difficult relationship with mother; parents often divorced

We use the outer ends of the eyebrows and the tip of the nose to determine set and positioning of the ears. **Average-set ears** are centered neatly between those two points. **High-set ears** tend to be higher than the outer ends of the eyebrows and higher than the tip of the nose. The tops of **low-set ears** fall lower than the outer ends of the eyebrows, and lower than the tip of the nose.

Those who have ears that are so long that they **begin above the eyebrows and end below the nose** will have success early in life that will last well into their late life.

Whenever I see people whose **right ear is considerably higher** than their left ear, I am quite sure that they were separated from their mother in their youth. The separation is often a physical separation such as abandonment or in divorce where the mother physically leaves the family and child. Though it can also be that the mother was so emotionally or spiritually unavailable that the child felt profoundly abandoned and was forced to live his life as though his mother did not exist.

It seems logical to assume that a higher left ear means that the father was missing from a child's life, but that's not the case. For one thing, I seldom see a significantly higher left ear, and when I do, there is usually no correlation with the ear positioning and any separation from the father in the early years. My guess is that historically children have not been (as) traumatized by their father's absence. Since earliest times, it was normal for fathers to be working the fields from sunup to sundown, and off hunting or warring for months or even years at a time, leaving them little time to interact with their children. Even in more modern times in most societies a good many fathers leave home before their children awaken and come home after they are asleep. Either for financial reasons, where many fathers must work two or more jobs to feed and clothe their families, or in the cases of driven and competitive executives who put in eighty or more hours a week, our lifestyle of absentee fathers hasn't changed much

Ear Set and Positioning

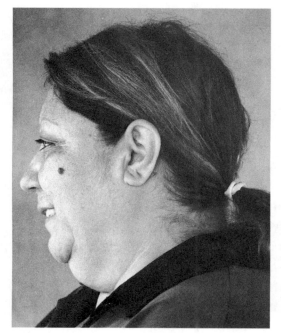

High-set ears

Low-set ears

over the centuries. And, therefore, because it seems so normal, children do not tend to be as traumatized by their absences—and their left ears do not rise higher on the sides of their heads.

Right ear higher than the left

Postitioning of Ears

forward facing	stubborn; selective hearing; intelligent; astute; likes attention, recognition, and admiration; clever; proud; assertive; trendsetter
flat to head	hypersensitive to sound, sensitive, shy, inconsistent, self-critical
set back	relies on intelligence
close to cheekbones	relies on basic instinct

If your ears are **forward facing** (they stand out from the sides of your head) you tend to hear only what you want to hear. When you were a kid on your way to hang out with your friends, and your mom told you to be home for dinner at five and not be late, all you heard was "be home for dinner." Somehow you just didn't hear the five and "don't be late" parts of her instructions. Not if you didn't want to hear it, that is. You've probably been called stubborn more times than you care to remember; but then again, that's what we're talking about, isn't it? Isn't it? . . . Did you "hear" that? If your ears do stick out from your head, you most likely won't notice when you're being teased, even here. But if you're a parent or partner to a forward-ear person, you're shaking your head and sighing right now.

Hearing only what you want to hear can keep you from being unduly influenced by others, which can be valuable in a myriad of circumstances. However, be careful not to discount others' valuable observations and opinions just because by nature you're willful. Use your gifts of intelligence, astuteness, and healthy pride to forward your opinions and causes. Since you enjoy being a trendsetter, don't alienate those who can give you the recognition and admiration that you like so much.

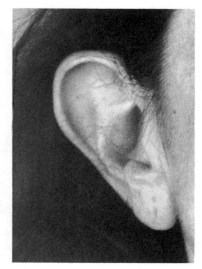

A forward-facing ear

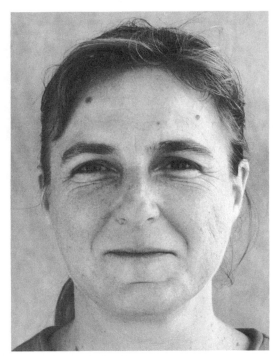

Ears set close to the head

Ears set back

The Chinese say a baby born with ears sticking out is born stubborn.

My ears are pretty **flat** to my head, which explains my ability to sit straight up from a deep sleep and mutter, "What's that noise?" There could be ten other people in the house and no one else will hear the normal patter of someone walking in the street three blocks away. It's not just that those of us with **ears flat to the head** are sensitive to sound, but we are hypersensitive to the point that normal sounds often sound like noise to us. Our friends and mates deserve much praise for changing seats with us in theaters or on buses and trains because we can't tolerate the chewing or tapping or whispering of those around us. The good news for sufferers like me is that I found acupuncture helped "cure" me of this affliction. My acupuncturist needled some prime kidney/Water points (remember, the ears and hearing are Water traits), and within a few weeks I noticed a significant difference. I am grateful that it helped so much, and so are those close to me.

Those of us with flat-to-the-head ears are often opposite from those with forward-facing ears in that we tend to listen too much to others' opinions. This can lead to unwarranted self-criticism. When I find myself falling into that natural trap, I remind myself to use my gift of confidence, which is apparent in my full cheeks.

Ears that are **set back,** farther from the cheekbones, reflect people who rely on their intelligence, more than their feelings, to sort their concerns, while someone with ears that are **closer to their cheekbones** relies more on their basic instincts. They know when things are right or wrong by their gut feelings.

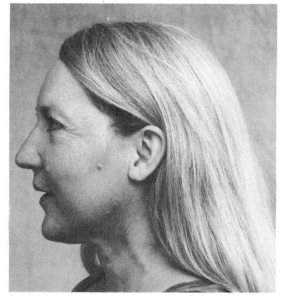

Ears set close to the cheekbones

Reading the External Ear

Besides looking at the size and shape of our ears, and their positioning on the sides of our head, we also examine the markings and colors of each part of the ear.

helix	the rim of the external ear
conch	the shell-like opening of the external ear
tragus	the flap between the conch and the cheekbone

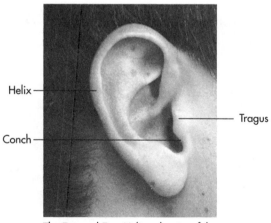

The External Ear: Helix—the rim of the external ear; Conch—the shell-like opening of the external ear; Tragus—the flap between the conch and the cheek

Markings on the Ears Relating to Early Childhood

In Part II in "The Specific Age Areas of the Face" and "Early-Age Markings on the Ears," we saw that the reactions to life-affecting events that occurred from ages one through fourteen are marked on the ears, most often on the helix, either by a line, a discoloration, a bump, an indentation, or a mole. (And that the left ear represents ages one through seven, and the right ear ages eight through fourteen, for males. The reverse is true for females: right ear represents ages one through seven, and the left ear ages eight through fourteen.)

The ears are the most difficult area of the face to read since many adults have vague or no memories of their early years. I am often fascinated by the replies that I get when I point out an ear marking and ask people if they remember a particular event that might have occurred at the matching age. Often they claim that nothing traumatic or out of the ordinary ever happened during their childhood. When I remind them that to a young child nearly every major change is distressing in some way, especially the birth of a sibling, moving to a new house, or changing schools or friends, there is frequently an eruption of emotions, some of which have been held back since childhood. Though people might be surprised by their reactions, I almost never am. Our early memories, though often difficult to access, have profound effects on us—mentally, emotionally, and spiritually. Mien Shiang is a valuable tool to help us find a balanced way to integrate our past and our present in order to have a healthier future.

Helix

round helix	common sense, lively, intellectual
too-thick helix	overindulgent
thin or no helix	extrovert, enthusiastic, restless, impulsive
too-thin helix w/no roundness	seeks for greater good, self-contained, needs yet avoids intimacy
pinched helix	insecurity
bumps on helix mark	abundant kidney Jing, especially at that age
vertical lines next to tragus	erratic parent, no stability in childhood

Markings such as scars, lines, and some discolorations are acquired, while others, such as moles and birthmarks, can be inherited.

Markings on the left or right sides of the face reveal father's or mother's influence as well as your own inner or outer personality and behavior.

When we describe the ideal ear, we also take into account the shape, size, and texture of the helix and the markings that appear there. The healthiest helix is evenly rounded at the top and sides, tapering off as it reaches the lobes. If you are lucky enough to have a **round helix,** then you are gifted with common sense and vitality, with a propensity for intellectual activity.

If the helix is **too thick,** you might have a penchant to overindulge in food and most pleasures, especially sexual pursuits. So be careful; too much of the good things can make you lazy!

Since the entire ear tells us about the state of our Jing, a **thin or nonexistent helix** lets us know that our Jing is relatively weak and needs to be nurtured and preserved regularly. Maybe because they have the challenge of Jing weakness, people with little or no helix can be somewhat overenthusiastic and restless, leading to impulsive behavior that can quickly turn aggressive when challenged.

A too-thin helix often represents someone who is concerned with the greater good of humankind, to the

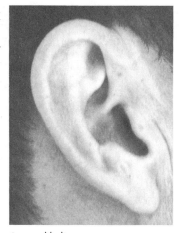

A round helix

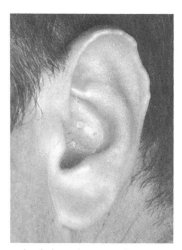

A thin helix with no roundness

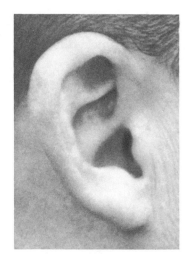

A thick helix

extent that they forgo their own needs and the needs of their loved ones. They can withdraw, going into their heads and becoming self-contained and self-involved as they try to save the world while ignoring their own personal life. They can grow to be less sexual because the pleasure of intimacy overwhelms them, making them feel guilty about ignoring their causes. If your helix is very thin, realize that stressful situations will make you want to isolate yourself, which hinders you more than helps you. Be especially careful not to overindulge in alcohol and drugs since they will contribute to more withdrawn behavior. Those proverbial long walks on the beach, treks in the woods, and meditation are great for your restlessness and impulsive tendencies.

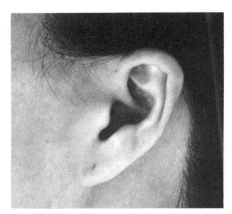

A pinched helix

When you see a **pinched helix** resembling the fluted edges of a pie crust, just off the top curve of the ear, you know that person is highly sensitive and has frequent bouts of insecurity, even when things are going well. This was the little child whose feelings were easily and often hurt, necessitating much reassurance and encouragement. Hopefully we outgrow our childhood insecurities, but the patterns are hard to break. If you have a pinched helix, remember to be patient with yourself and to look for the kind intentions of others before assuming an insult has been offered. If you have a child with a pinched helix, again be patient. It won't help to tell him to be a big boy, or to ignore the hurts; he needs a couple extra hugs and big reassurances that he is a good guy, capable of weathering the tough spots in life. Teach him creative ways to deal with the inevitable upsets that come with being human.

Many people have little **bumps** on their helix. They represent abundant kidney Jing, especially at that age mark. When I see this bump in people past the age indicated, I ask them what happened to them then. Almost always, I'm told of a traumatic event, and almost as frequently they claim that they don't know how they got through the trauma, that they suddenly had a strength or endurance greater than they had had before or after the event. That's the kidney Jing, I tell them. One woman asked me if the little bumps of cellulite on

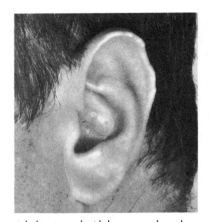

A helix marred with bumps and notches

her thighs were evidence that she would get a little boost of kidney Jing in her later life. I wish I could have told her it was true.

It's hard to pull the wool over the eyes of those who have what I call built-in, automatic lie detectors—those **little vertical lines right next to the tragus.** These were children who had erratic parenting with little or no stability when they were children. Either their mom or dad, or both parents, would regularly threaten them with punishments that never came or confuse them with the opposite tack, telling them, "I'm only punishing you harshly because I love you." Children who recognized the empty threats or learned that they were being punished harshly because their mom or dad was responding to her or his own anger developed those little vertical lines.

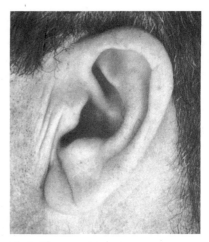

Vertical lines next to the tragus

Ear Color

No matter one's race or natural coloring, the **normal healthy color** of your ears tends to be a bit **lighter** than your facial complexion, although it is not unusual for a healthy person to have their ears match their face in tone and color.

ears lighter than face	normal, healthy
ears darker than face	stagnation, sluggish temperament
red ears	irritable, thin-skinned, intelligent, high blood pressure
red, dry, scaly ears	irritable, unforgiving
gray ears	talkative, inattentive
suddenly gray ears	sudden illness, misfortune
earlobes too red	ruled by passions, excitable
earlobes too pale	passionless, ruled by head
cold, pale ears	nervous temperament, anxious

If your ears are always **darker** than your face, it indicates that you have a sluggish temperament. As you perk up physically, emotionally, and spiritually, you will notice that your ears will gradually lighten in color.

Your ears might get **red** when you are embarrassed or are experiencing other heightened emotions such as anger, anxiety, or sexual excitement. But if your ears are always redder than your face, you are probably easily irritated and thin-skinned. Since you are also intelligent, it would be a good idea to contemplate why your feelings are so easily hurt; it could help you to reduce your irritability and even your propensity to develop high blood pressure.

You might know someone who has chronic **red, dry, scaly ears.** Do they seem to be self-centered, to the point of being compassionless and unforgiving? These people are so irritated by everything and everyone that they have lost their sense of belonging to the world—to their family or friends or community. They use their intellect to separate themselves from others, but mostly to separate themselves from their own emotional and spiritual pain. They need to be brought back with kindness and patience to the point where they can empathize with others and, in turn, learn to love themselves, warts and all.

Gray ears are a teacher's nightmare since it's nearly impossible to focus the gray-eared person's attention. These people just love to chat on and on, flitting from one subject to another, without seeming to take a breath. I often think, while I'm trying to have my quiet morning cup of coffee at my neighborhood café, that cell phones were invented especially for the gray-eared people. See for yourself—if you can get the phone pried from their ears.

If your ears are not normally gray, but **suddenly** turn so, the ancients said that you needed to be alert for the onset of a sudden illness, or misfortune. I have never seen this, but some of my students are keeping an eye out for this quick color change in their clinic and private-patient practices.

The color of the earlobes can give you a quick insight into people's passions. If the lobes are **too red,** these excitable people never listen to their head when it comes to love, and their hearts are probably broken quite often. On the other hand, if their ears are **too pale,** you know that they are ruled by their heads, and never by their hearts. Passion is not a vital part of their life. If **pale ears are also cold,** then an anxious and nervous temperament further keeps them from surrendering to, or even noticing, passions.

Earlobes

The fatter the earlobe, the fatter the purse.
OLD CHINESE SAYING

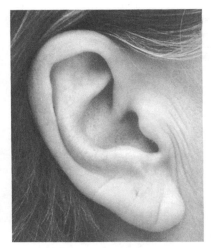

Long earlobes

Earlobes are key indicators of longevity and wealth. The ancient Taoists said that it took wealth to live a long and healthy life, and sadly that is still a reality in today's world. That's why you see many Chinese grandfathers from the old country pulling gently on their grandchildren's earlobes. They are continuing a venerable tradition of helping the little ones to develop **bigger** and **longer lobes** to increase their potential for a long life and financial security in old age.

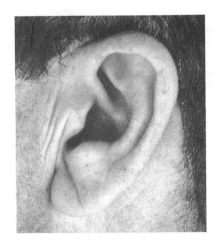

Big earlobes

long lobes	long life, wisdom, good wealth potential
big lobes	good planning for the future
thick and dangling lobes	idealistic, forceful, money comes easily, extravagant
short lobes	scattered, impatient, emotional
short and thin lobes	present-oriented, difficulty with money
soft, delicate lobes	refined, little vitality, seeks gentle relationships, isolates self
fleshy lobes	connected to the earth
fleshy, pink lobes	lively, sensual, witty, jealous
attached lobes	attached to family (who raised them), impulsive

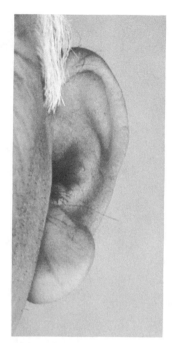

Thick and dangling earlobes

While **long lobes** are auspicious with their promise of long life, wisdom, and great wealth potential, lobes that are **thick** and **dangling** mean that money might come too easily and spell financial disaster. People who do not know how to earn money frequently don't know how to manage money. When they suddenly come into wealth through inheritance, gifts, or chance, they stand a high probability of losing that money by being big spenders and overindulging their family and friends. A surprising percentage of big lottery winners claim that their huge windfalls were actually disastrous to their relationships with family and friends, and they deeply regret their "good luck." It makes me wonder what their lobes look like.

Short lobes come with the challenges of being scattered, impatient, and emotional. Always remember that there are two sides to every trait, and seek the creative attributes associated with each one.

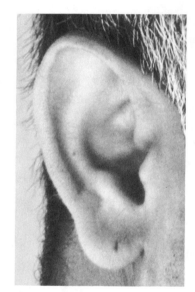

Short earlobes

We know that long lobes represent the gift of longevity, so if you have short earlobes, be conscious of taking good care of yourself. There is no doubt that you can turn your challenge into a healthy, long, prosperous life—you'll just have to work harder at it than your long-lobed brethren.

People with **short, thin earlobes** are present-oriented; it's hard for them to plan for the future. And because they don't make money easily, they can become obsessed with it, even to the point of greed. Each time I teach about the earlobes, I know someone will inevitably point out that I have short and thin earlobes and wonder aloud if that means that I will die young, impoverished, and greedy; and if so, doesn't that frighten me? I assure my students that they don't have to worry. My short and thin lobes simply remind me that I have to work for my money and force myself to plan for my future, even though I find long-range planning tedious. And though I love good food (way too much of it), I take care of myself by eating healthily, exercising moderately, and trying not to let stress overwhelm me. Good advice for anyone, but a little more important for those of us with little lobes.

Soft, delicate earlobes belong to those with refined minds, but little vitality. They overly romanticize the simplest relationship, yet tend never to act upon their feelings. They would rather live in the fantasy than be disappointed by the reality. Obviously, living in a romantic fantasy world can lead to isolation and sexual inhibitions. If these "romanticizers" do marry, it will be a gently loving relationship with few demands. A client of mine has a cousin who writes romance novels and fits this description to a T. I would love to check the earlobes of all the famous romance novelists and see if that holds true.

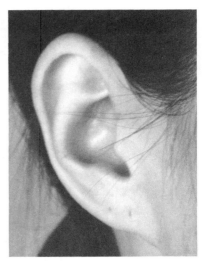

Soft, delicate, short, and thin earlobes

Nice **fleshy** (more plump than thick) **earlobes** indicate closeness to the earth, often literally. Fleshy-lobed people have beautiful gardens. These are not people who wear gardening gloves; they love to squeeze the rich, moist earth between their fingers. A couple years ago I was scheduled to give a seminar to a group of lawyers in an exclusive downtown Los Angeles high-rise. When I walked into the stately boardroom, there sat fifteen attorneys around an immense mesquite table inlaid with smooth chunks of copper. The scene was just as I expected it to be for a group of lawyers, but what surprised me was that about two-thirds of the attorneys had nice, big fleshy earlobes. When I mentioned that I usually only saw earlobes like that on farmers, gardeners, or real estate agents, they laughed and then told me they were real estate attorneys! Fleshy lobes seldom lie.

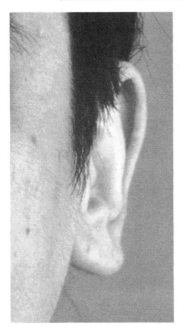

Fleshy earlobes

Attached earlobes are lobes that do not hang free. They are attached directly, usually at an angle, to the side of the neck. When we say these people are attached to the family they were born into, we do not mean they necessarily get along with their parents or siblings. I have a fortysomething friend with attached earlobes who calls her mother, who also has attached earlobes, in New York every morning from her home in Los Angeles, and every morning they have a huge argument. Each morning squabble is loud and lively, but nothing is ever resolved because they're not arguing

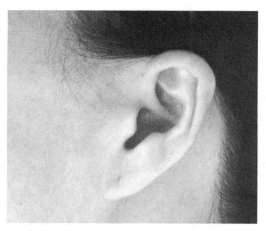
Attached earlobes

about anything specific. They are using their mutual repressed anger and impulsiveness to stay attached to each other, because that's their nature.

Each cares very much what the other thinks of her, and how she feels. Though they seldom agree and frequently upset each other, neither would consider limiting their contact to only once a week, or even every other day. They make each other miserable, but they are comfortable in their misery—as long as they stay attached.

Ear Cartilage and Your Basic Constitution

Pinch the body of your ear, not the lobe, but anywhere else on the outside ear. Does it feel firm and tight, or is the cartilage of your ear soft and pliable? The tighter and firmer the cartilage, the stronger your basic constitution.

Firm cartilage does not mean physical strength.

tight and firm ear cartilage	strong constitution
fragile ear cartilage	fragile constitution
too tight or firm cartilage	inflexible

Tight and firm ear cartilage might explain your ability to bounce back quickly from illness or adversity. You have a natural gift of a robust, enduring basic constitution.

If your cartilage is **fragile,** you most likely have a fragile constitution. You need to take better care of yourself when illness strikes or when under stress. You cannot push your luck and expect to bounce right back to optimum health; you have to nurture yourself to get better.

Sometimes a lot is too much. If the ear cartilage is **too tight or firm,** it might be a sign of imbalance, an inability to be flexible in mind, body, and spirit. In some types it can be a helpful warning, such as a precursor to stroke, among other things.

My own ears, while on the smaller side, are quite tight and firm, and I do have a great natural ability to weather ailments and difficulties. I'm hardly ever ill, and when I do get something minor, it's usually over within a few days. Of course I have had my share of grief and other emotional setbacks, and when I succumb, it can be deep and extremely painful, but I do rally after a short period and seldom am I out of commission for long.

I inherited my strong constitution from my mother, yet our disposition toward illness couldn't have been more different. Though I have been blessed with good physical health, my mother had many serious illnesses during her life, as well as a myriad of uncommon complications connected to those illnesses. Her tight, firm ear cartilage didn't protect her from ill health or complications, but it certainly explained her ability to recover, over and over, from these serious conditions that often did fell others.

HAIRLINE

socialization fear Water kidney black/blue early adolescence

Was your adolescent family life like Ozzie and Harriet's, or closer to the Osbournes'? Were you a good little girl or boy who always obeyed and never argued, or were you naturally rebellious?

The shape, width, consistency, and symmetry of the hairline tells us how well socialized we were by our parents during those adolescent years. We use the term *socialized* to mean how you responded to your parents' jurisdiction and influence. Since the kidney Jing is responsible for our growth cycles, including puberty, this is a significant Water element feature that reflects an emotional time for most early teens (and their parents).

ALWAYS CONSIDER THE **WATER ELEMENT** ASSOCIATIONS FOR THE **HAIRLINE**

characteristic	socialization
emotion	fear
element	Water
organ	kidney
color	black/blue
ages	early adolescence

A hairline that is nearly as wide as the middle part of the forehead and flows smoothly in a small arc without jagged edging, bumps, or indentations is considered the Taoist **ideal hairline.**

even/symmetrical hairline	good socialization
exceptionally even hairline	repression
uneven hairline	difficulties due to parental stresses during early youth
narrow hairline	heavily socialized, conforming
shadowing along hairline	very socialized
indentations on hairline	more introverted
bump on hairline	more social
medium-wide hairline	more independent
very wide hairline	rebellious
Veil of Tears/wispy hairs	difficulty feeling and expressing true feelings
protruding ridge above hairline	psychic, receives information

If you were lucky to have little emotional trauma during puberty, or if you didn't internalize the negative effects of any emotional traumas of that time, the more **even** and **symmetrical** your hairline will be. By *even* we don't mean shape; a curved, squared, or straight-across hairline could be either even or uneven. If the hairline is a smooth line, it is considered to be even. If it is jagged or erratic-looking, we consider this to be **uneven.**

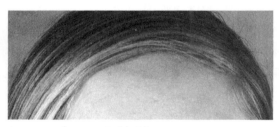

An even and symmetrical hairline

An uneven hairline

Though we say that an **even hairline** represents "good socialization" and can indicate a healthy and nontraumatic adolescence, it does not always mean that the adolescent years were easy or uneventful. If you have an even hairline although your adolescence was filled with family chaos, it could be that you were able to detach and identify more closely with your peers than with your parents. If those peer relationships were caring and supportive, it was easier to distance yourself and not be overwhelmed by the turmoil of your family life.

An **exceptionally even** hairline might suggest repression, pointing to the adolescent who was afraid, or not allowed, to rebel and confront her parents in a healthy manner. Anytime you sublimate your true feelings, you risk losing your true sense of self. This leads to behavior that is fearful, repressed, and docile. If that was your adolescent situation, it is important for you to unbury those feelings, experience them, and then let them go. I know it isn't as easy as that sounds; bringing up old hurts is painful. But isn't it better to finally acknowledge and experience the horrible lurking pain that is always with you, no matter how deeply you think you've buried it, if it means that you can finally release that pain forever? No matter how long it has been, it is never too late to become healthier and happier.

One of my university students was profoundly moved to do just this following our study of the traits of the hairline. After admitting to her deeply buried hurts, reexperiencing them in a safe environment, and then releasing them through therapy, acupuncture treatment, and specific Qi Gong exercises, her perfectly even hairline actually got a little ragged on her right side. She told us that it made sense to her that it was on her right side since it was her mother who had inhibited her natural independence, encouraging her to always act—to the *outside* world—like a "perfect lady" with no outward betrayal of her true feelings. Right after she had a long series of talks with her mother wherein she found the courage to disagree with her about certain past issues, her hairline started to get jagged. Her eighty-two-year-old mother, who has a razor-sharp hairline, at first fought her daughter tooth and nail, doing everything in her power to keep the events of the past in the past. But her daughter persisted, and her mother was eventually thrilled when they finally found a common ground and mended their relationship. My student's mother even sent me a touching note saying that it's her goal to get her own hairline "a little messed up"!

If you strictly conformed to the wishes of your parents during puberty, you most likely have a **narrow hairline** as well as difficulty standing up for yourself. You are used to agreeing with others, especially those who have authority over

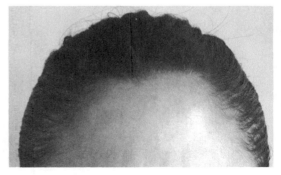

A narrow hairline

you, such as an employer, landlord, or teacher, so as not to rock the boat. Our parents are supposed to teach us and prepare us to separate from them in a healthy manner, to cultivate our own well-thought-out opinions even when they differ from theirs, and to go into our adult lives with confidence and courage. If the opposite happens, and we are taught that we are bad or ungrateful, or not smart enough to lead our own lives under our own terms, it's difficult to learn on our own how to be confident and courageous and stand up to other authority figures, or even equals. If you have a narrow hairline and this behavioral description fits you, find where your greatest strengths lie, and work hard at developing them. For instance, if you have a good strong nose, exploit those natural gifts of ego, leadership, and drive to overcome your oversocialization. If you have a great strong jaw, use that determination to push yourself to stand up for yourself, to challenge others when appropriate, and to have faith in your own ideas, wants, and emotions. You could also try what one of my students did a couple years ago. She had her hairline widened by electrolysis. Simply because she was determined enough to do this (she has great jaws), it helped her immensely. I have definitely seen a marked improvement in her confidence in the last couple years.

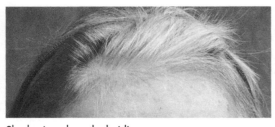

Shadowing along the hairline

Other indications of oversocialization are **shadowing** and **indentations** along the hairline. The shadowing is usually a brownish or blue tone to the skin either just below or along the hairline and tells us that these people have had a difficult time asserting themselves most of their lives. The indentations are often hard to see, but noticeable to the touch, which makes it tricky to detect their presence in others since people with hairline indentations are often shy and introverted and do not like to be touched unless they feel familiar and safe with you.

The opposite of indentations on the hairline is little **bumps,** also often noticed only by touch, and these indicate someone who loves the social life. I have both an indentation and a bump on my hairline. The indentation is on the right side, which indicates that I would be somewhat introverted and shy in my behavior, while the bump on my left side indicates a desire to be outgoing. Let's see how we can explain the contradiction from a Mien Shiang point of view. Remember that the right side of our face represents both our mother's influence and how we present ourselves to the outside world, and our left side represents our father's influence and our innermost thoughts and emotions. Since both my parents were quite sociable, especially during my youth, and neither pushed me nor discouraged me to be social, let's then consider the inner and outer aspects of those markings. I was an adolescent who had an active imagination but was much too shy to easily jump into friendships or even informal groups. Yet there was a strong inner desire not just to be connected to others, but to be so in an outgoing, fun, and social way. What a dilemma—shy on the outside and amusing and perky on the inside.

The truth is, that's still how I am. But long ago my inner desire to play and have fun with the other kids was stronger than my equally introverted nature. The loneliness turned out to be worse than the fear of rejection, I'm happy to say. The worry of taking a chance is still there, but experience has taught me that it is well worth it. If my parents had known about face reading during my youth, they could have understood my inherent contradictory desires and helped me to find a happy balance.

A **medium-wide hairline** is preferable as it indicates someone who rebelled against parental authority at the appropriate age and in a healthy manner. If that's your hairline, then you learned in your youth to question rules and others' opinions and to trust your own feelings and instincts and then to make appropriately indepen-

dent decisions about your life and the world around you. Yet, if your hairline is **very wide,** you might just have been naturally rebellious to any normal parental authority, and you could still as an adult have issues with following orders and direction. It's a good bet you like to work alone or be in charge. Keep your sense of humor when you find yourself getting annoyed at those who don't want to fol-

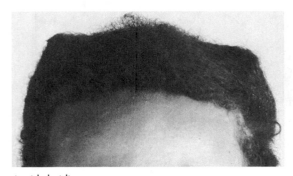

A wide hairline

low your authority—especially if those rebels also have wide foreheads!

The **little wispy hairs** that some people have along their hairline are what I call the Veil of Tears. Those delicate hairs act as a veil, hiding the true shape of the hairline, just as these people hide their true feelings when they are hurt. I've found that those with the Veil of Tears are not naturally disposed to be misleading about their feelings, but rather they learned to put on a happy face as adolescents because the consequences of expressing their hurt or fear relating to their family situation were too dire.

The ancients believed that those who have a **protruding ridge above their hairline** are psychic and receive information from the spirits. Now that it's popular

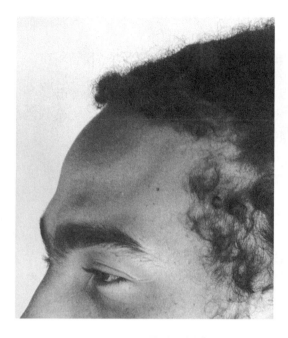

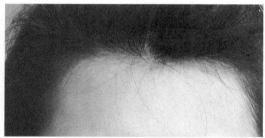

The short, curled hairs in the first photo and the short, wispy hairs along the hairline in the second are both examples of the Veil of Tears.

for men to shave their heads (and some women, too), we get to actually see these ridges more often. All the people who have this ridge whom I've asked if they consider themselves psychic or at least exceptionally intuitive have answered undoubtedly yes.

Hairline Shapes

Unless you wear your hair closely cropped without bangs, or it's all pulled back from your face, or you shave your head, it's difficult for others to know the true shape of your hairline. The strictly defined hairline shapes such as a widow's peak, a straight line zipping across the forehead, or the perfect top half of an oval often stand out because so many of us have undefined hairlines reaching back on one side only, or the sneaky male-pattern-baldness shape—or as one student calls it, the increasingly shapeless hairline shape.

widow's peak/heart-shaped	desirability in women, traditional, sensual, charismatic
M-shaped hairline	desirability in men, creative, perceptive, affectionate
curved hairline	motivated by money, gracious, good bosses
square hairline	mostly on men, reliable, follow direction, need recognition
receding hairline	success in love, money, virility
clover hairline (high middle)	hard workers, not ambitious, hard luck

When the ancient Taoist match-makers went on their searches for potential wives for their wealthy clients' sons, the **heart-shaped widow's peak** was high on the list of most desirable physical traits, especially since those with widow's peaks are very traditional women, as well as sensual and charis-

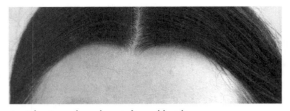

A widow's peak, or heart-shaped hairline

matic. Those were indeed the top requirements for a good wife in those times. It's the perfect hairline in our present time for the professional corporate wife, as these women can easily fit into nearly any relationship or situation, and they thrive in hierarchical relationships. Since they feel unsettled by nature, they enjoy the challenge of being uprooted by the demands of their husband's moving up the corporate ladder, and back and forth across the country every couple years or so. (That can be true, too, for the stay-at-home dad who enjoys following his corporate wife from city to city as she advances in her career, but I've noticed that he doesn't usually have a widow's peak.)

There seems to be fewer women with widow's peaks compared to fifty or sixty years ago. In fact, several times a student has told me that she looks exactly like her mother, or grandmother—except that she has not inherited her widow's peak. I cannot help but wonder how influential our collective behavior has been in redefining the hairline.

Men with widow's peaks are equally traditional in their values and lifestyles, but the only hierarchical relationship they enjoy is when they are at the top of the hierarchy. Though they are as sensual and charismatic as their female counterparts, the man with a widow's peak doesn't lose his sense or appearance of masculinity. Popular actor Andy Garcia is a great example of a sensual, masculine man with a widow's peak.

The most desirable hairline for men is said to be the **classic M-shape,** since these men are considered strong leaders and protectors, as well as being affectionate,

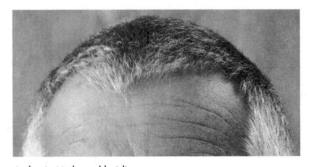

A classic M-shaped hairline

attentive, creative, perceptive, loving, and sensual lovers. That's a pretty attractive list of traits.

A good many of the macho film heroes of the last couple generations, such as John Wayne, Marlon Brando, and Robert Mitchum, had the classic M-shaped hairline.

When women have the M-shape, they do often have more of what are considered "masculine" traits and behaviors, and while they have great success in business, they tend to have difficulties in romantic relationships. It's unfortunate that our society still insists on locking men and women into strict rules of behavior, especially in love.

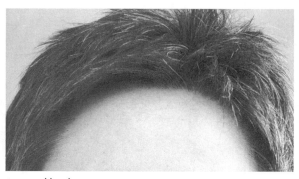
A curved hairline

If you are looking for employment, you might want to check out your future boss's hairline while you are interviewing. Your best bet might be one with a **curved hairline,** since they are fair to their employees, gracious in business and social settings, and motivated by financial matters. The reverse is true, too: If you are looking for an employee to help run your company, you couldn't go wrong with a nicely curved–hairline candidate.

If you're not looking for a leader, but want a team player who is reliable, conscientious, and follows orders and directions to a T, then the man with a **square-shaped hairline** is the one for you. Just remember to consistently give him his due recognition or else he will become discouraged, even depressed. His loyalty will pay off in many ways, including longevity in the company since he likes to stay close to the family he was born to and will pass up more pay and prestige to stay put and not move up, or away. When I say *he* in this case, I definitely mean men, as it's rare to find a woman with a square hairline. Interestingly, the woman with the widow's peak hairline often fits this same description.

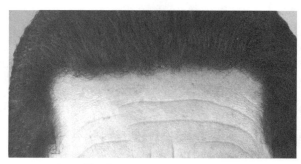
A square-shaped hairline

There has hardly been a class or seminar that I've held in which some nice-looking man with a **receding hairline** hasn't flinched or groaned audibly the minute I introduced the subject of hairlines. To the ancient Taoist monks a receding hairline was a sign of good luck because it hopefully meant the man was going to become completely bald. That usually elicits an even louder groan from my student until I explain that to the ancients not only was baldness a handsome trait, but it foretold of success in all aspects of life, especially in love and money and virility. It's one of my goals to get American and European men to change their prejudice about being bald. It isn't my goal to change women's attitudes since I've found that most women really do think that bald is beautiful—and for pretty much the same reasons the ancient Taoists did.

One hairline you might want to avoid for all reasons is the **three-leaf-clover hairline,** which has three curves, the highest in the middle. Thank goodness this is quite rare (I think I've seen only one), as this person simply has hard luck all around. Since they don't have intellectual curiosity, or much ambition of any kind, they tend to find sporadic physical labor that will give them just enough money for their essentials. Probably because of this sporadic lifestyle and general malaise of mind, body, and spirit, they often have serious health problems beginning in their early thirties.

FOREHEAD

parental influence fear Water kidney black/blue adolescence through mid 20s

To those of us who live in the Western world, the forehead has to be the least attention-getting or adorned part of our faces. We put jewelry on our ears and noses and through our lips and eyebrows; we paint our lips, cheeks, eyebrows, eyelids, and even our lashes. And even though we don't adorn or paint our jaws and chins, they are more "out there" than the forehead. Covering the jaws and chin with hair adds to the awareness of those features, while hair covering the forehead detracts from or even seems to eliminate the feature. You can't jut out your forehead the way you can your chin to demonstrate authority and dominance, or clench your forehead the way you do your jaws to betray tension and anger. Even forehead wrinkling actually comes from raising or narrowing the eyebrows.

One Nebraska man feels that his forehead is such a waste of face that he recently sold advertising space there to a snoring-remedy company for one month for $37,375 (January 2005). His novel idea has sparked a few imitators, but I have a feeling this is a fad with a short life.

*In 2004 former Soviet leader Mikhail Gorbachev
petitioned to trademark his forehead birthmark
after a Russian vodka company began using a
facsimile of his famous birthmark on its
bottle labels.*

When I was a little girl in New England and had trouble making up my mind between two toys, or which of two friends to play with, my mother would slice open an apple and then press an apple seed onto each side of my forehead. Each seed represented one of the two conflicting choices. The seed that stayed on longest represented the winner of the dilemma. When I got older, my friends and I would stick an apple seed to our forehead, then recite the alphabet. The seed was supposed to fall off when you reached the first letter of the first name of your one true love. My first big crush's name was Peter, and I was heartbroken that my apple seeds never stayed stuck to my forehead for the recitation of sixteen long letters. (There may have been something to it, since Peter and I never did get together.)

So just what can we read on the inexpressive, unrented, unadorned, untrademarked, and often unseen forehead?

Lots, as it turns out.

To begin with, the size and shape of our forehead tells us about our *inherited* issues regarding intelligence, emotion, and perception.

*The forehead skin is the thickest facial skin and is
rich in sebaceous glands and sweat glands.*

The Three Regions

THE FOREHEAD IS DIVIDED INTO THREE REGIONS

Heaven: upper forehead	intelligence	aptitude for rational thought, noble sentiments, generosity
Human: middle forehead	emotional	parental influence, morality, common sense, security
Earth: lower forehead	intuition	insight based on experience, realistic, sensual

The three horizontal regions of the forehead are labeled in the Taoist tradition as Heaven, Human, and Earth, with each region telling us something specific about our ancestral and parental inherited issues.

The **ideal forehead** is smooth and of ample height and breadth, and all three regions are equally domed. But, if the top third of your forehead, the **Heaven region,** is more prominent—rounder, broader, or higher—than the other two areas, we know that your most exceptional inherited gift from your ancestors is your intelligence and aptitude for rational thought. Your family and friends benefit greatly from your generosity and noble sentiments.

Your brother might have a more domed or a wider middle area of his forehead—his **Human region**—telling us that his special inherited gift is his ability to have healthy and appropriate emotions. He has a strong sense of morality, which was directly influenced by your parents' own personal ethics. People instinctively rely on his commonsense approach to life and advice, and to the sense of security that he creates for himself and those near and dear to him.

And your sister could have a more prominent lower forehead—her **Earth region**—which helps her to trust her natural intuition, enabling her to learn from her personal experiences. Her interesting combination of sensuality and no-nonsense realism draws others to her.

Our foreheads also record our relationships with our parents during our teens through early twenties. This is a significant Water element time in our development, as it is when we take what we have learned from our parents and begin to apply that knowledge as young adults, free to make our own life decisions. Very few people have no lines on their foreheads because this is such an exciting as well as tumultuous time of life.

ALWAYS CONSIDER THE **WATER ELEMENT** ASSOCIATIONS FOR THE **FOREHEAD**

characteristic	parental influence
emotion	fear
element	Water
organ	kidney
color	black/blue
ages	adolescence through midtwenties

Size and Shape

prominent forehead	in their minds, strong, persevering, egalitarian
broad or wide forehead	broad focus and interests, good memory, learned, inconstant
narrow forehead	narrow focus and interests, heavily socialized, conforming
high forehead	intelligent, forward thinker, good concentration
disproportionately high forehead	detached from real life and problems
low forehead	realist, down-to-earth, deliberate
extremely low forehead	unadventurous, unhurried
flat forehead	observant, serious, analytical, quick learner, likes the facts
slanted forehead	deal maker, mediator, must be in charge
convex forehead	curious, quick, agile mind, multitasker, easily bored
rounded forehead	imaginative, dreamy, inventive
many protuberances	dynamic, hyperactive, big temper

Men tend to have sloping foreheads, while women have straighter foreheads.

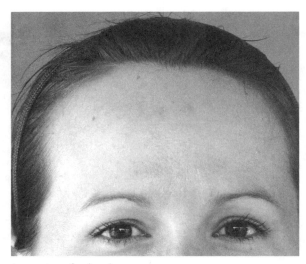

A prominent forehead

People who have **prominent foreheads** in comparison to the rest of their face spend lots of time in their head, thinking, imagining, and analyzing. These are strong-minded people with gifts of perseverance and egalitarianism. Doesn't Albert Einstein fit this description perfectly?

A **wide or broad forehead** equals a broad range of knowledge. These jack-of-all-trades people can help you in any number of ways, and they very much enjoy lending you a hand as well as an opinion. The big picture is their forte; they examine any event or situation in its totality and from every angle. Just don't torture them with the details; they hate the details. Their love of learning and their great memories makes them fascinating conversationalists, not to mention fantastic Trivial Pursuit partners. The downside is that they can be all over the map and never focus long or intensely enough on one subject or talent to further their lives in the ways they desire. And, those broad ranges of interests that lead to so many varied and exciting experiences can lead to an inconstant character, especially regarding their passions and sexual behavior. Sometimes too much really *is* too much.

A wide forehead

As you would expect, a **narrow forehead** equals a narrow range of interest. These detail-oriented people are interested in only one or two specific things or themes, which are often intricately related to each other. They often are the experts in obscure, highly detailed subjects that require intense attention to minutiae. A while ago I visited a lab at UCLA where they are conducting groundbreaking research on the human genome theory and noticed that the scientists who were the visionaries, who wondered at the big picture of humanity and had created this cutting-edge university department,

A broad forehead

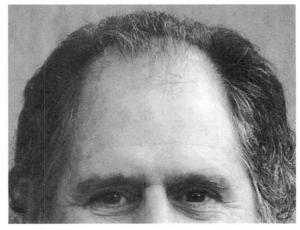

A narrow forehead

A high forehead

all had very wide foreheads. The researchers who resembled the stereotypical scientist, with their heads bent over their microscopes and computers, completely enthralled with their studies and absolutely unaware of our presence, all had narrow foreheads—a perfect fit for their narrow, high-tech instruments on the long, narrow tables they labored over. Whether broad or narrow, every single one of them had a **high forehead,** depicting their intelligence, ability to concentrate, and forward-thinking mind. A few even had **disproportionately high foreheads,** a sure sign of someone who tends to be very detached from the real problems of the world. I'll bet those were the researchers who forget to eat or pay their bills and miss more meetings and social functions than they attend. Their mates might care, but they seldom do.

Most people I know with **low foreheads** don't like to make quick decisions. Their realistic nature encourages them to use their down-to-earth sensibilities to deliberate long and hard and come to a fair and equitable conclusion. It may take them a while to form their opinion, but once formed, it's hard to budge them to another point of view.

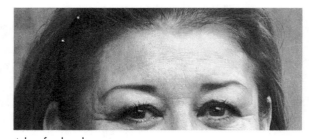
A low forehead

You won't see many scientists or other creative professionals with **extremely low foreheads,** as these people are mired in reality and have little use for the innovative life. They can be deliberate and basic; their work and lives in general are practical and functional. These ultrarealists don't care for the frills. A job is taken for the money, to provide themselves and their family with the essentials, rather than for the excitement or creativity of the work.

Two brothers founded a successful and innovative business several years ago, and though their names and their voices are nearly identical, their foreheads give an immediate inkling to their very different personalities.

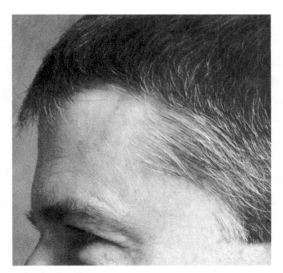

A flat forehead

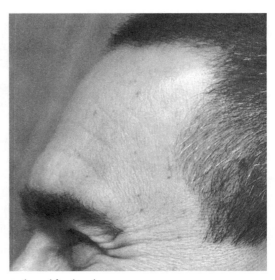

A slanted forehead

The older brother has a decidedly **flat and slanted forehead,** and true to our Taoist classification, he is an observant and analytical man of temperate behavior who approaches each new circumstance with staid determination to quickly learn every aspect of the situation and then find a sensible solution. His brother, on the other hand, the one with the nicely **convex forehead,** has a quick and agile mind and is excited and curious about everything. Since he likes to have several balls in the air at all times, he never says no to taking on a new, interesting challenge, no matter how jammed his calendar seems to be. Understandably, his problem is completion. Finishing projects can be boring; he'd rather throw even more balls up in the air and see where they fall.

What eventually happens is that the two brothers put their heads—flat and convex—together to provide a balance to each other, finding a practical and inspired

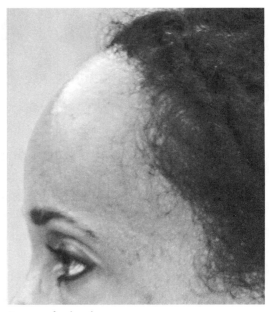

A convex forehead

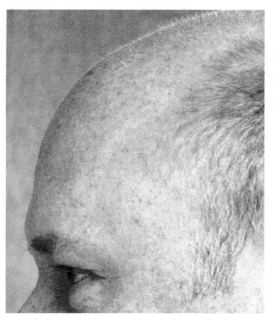
A round forehead

solution that neither could have reached on their own. It's no wonder they are successful and enjoy working together so much.

The **rounded forehead** is not as pronounced as the convex one. A few years ago I gave a seminar to a group of animators at a major film studio and noticed that the majority of the animators had very round foreheads. "You're quite an imaginative group, obviously," I said upon greeting them. "Your foreheads tell me that most of you had imaginary friends when you were little."

"We still do," answered one of the men with a laugh.

What a perfect job for the imaginative, dreamy, and inventive personality that goes with the rounded forehead.

Every once in a while you will see someone with many **protuberances,** little knobby lumps and bumps, on their forehead. Though these people can have dynamic personalities, they are tricky to be around since their full-of-life, life-of-the-party behavior can quickly escalate to hyperactive temper outbursts. Since you probably won't know why they're suddenly angry, you have a good chance of unwittingly making things worse if you try to "talk some sense" to them. Quietly extricate yourself from their presence before their tantrum becomes violent.

Markings on the Forehead

Markings on the forehead, such as moles, scars, lines, and discolorations, tell a story about your teenage years through your midtwenties. To help you get used to noting the placement and meanings of markings on the face, let's use a few real examples.

At a recent Mien Shiang workshop that I gave in Venice, California, several attendees had great stories on their foreheads.

Peter had a nicely domed forehead, which I would expect as he is a thirty-four-year-old, highly talented, innovative designer and department head at a top

Markings such as scars, lines, and some discolorations are acquired, while others, such as moles and birthmarks, can be inherited.

Markings on the left or right sides of the face reveal father's or mother's influence as well as your own inner or outer personality and behavior.

Fortune 500 company. His forehead didn't have a lot of markings, but he did have one straight, deep line that ran right across his forehead at the age points of nineteen, twenty, and twenty-one, plainly dividing his upper and lower forehead. It was evident to me that he had had a profoundly intense change in his life wherein he had dramatically broken with the past and entered a new future that was in every way—mentally, spiritually, and physically—severed from his "old" life. Peter looked amazed, then nodded and told us that around that age he had left home and come out publicly as a gay man, and his life did indeed change in every way imaginable. It was a wonderfully empowering and exciting time for him, but there was also a poignant sense of leaving one familiar and happy life for a completely different one; he had countless complex feelings to accompany him on his journey. Since Peter was being so open with our group, I decided to ask him about a little round scar on the left side (which represents his father's influence and his own inner emotions) of his forehead around the age of sixteen to seventeen. He smiled knowingly. That was when he had confided to his father that he was gay, he told us, and that experience with his loving and supportive father was one of the most profound of his life, to this day.

At this same workshop, Anna, a thirty-five-year-old dancer, had a mole nestled on her uneven hairline next to the fifteen-year-old position. She recalled for us in a soft voice that as she was packing to leave for New York to join the American Ballet Theatre, one of the world's most prestigious ballet troupes, her father changed his mind. He could not allow his fifteen-year-old daughter to leave the family, even though that meant she would never be the prima ballerina she believed she was meant to be. To this day, Anna feels that decision has affected every aspect of her life and is one for which she is still seeking resolution.

One of our workshop guests asked a great question: Was the mole present before or after Anna's fifteenth year, or more specifically, before or after the decision that changed her life?

In the study of Mien Shiang we observe that a mark can be a result of a momentous event (acquired), or we might be born with a facial marking (inherited). When the marking is inherited, we note the age-related placement on the face and consider that marking a forewarning of a momentous event later in life. The same holds true for acquired markings that occur before you reach the age indicated by the scar or other marking.

Again, I want to remind you that a momentous occurrence does not have to be negative, but most of us have experienced that major life-affecting events are often accompanied by some challenges or difficulties. The term *growing pains* is an apt description that most of us identify with. At the same time, expect the unexpected, like our friend Peter, whose facial marking foretold a life-changing experience, and that event was a profoundly positive experience from the onset. And, incidentally, he received the scar when he was about six years old, falling out of a tree.

We all have events in our lives that leave their marks, and those marks act as wonderful alerts to give us a "heads-up" to prepare for the inevitable changes in our lives. They don't tell us exactly what the change will be or exactly how it will affect us, but they do give us a hint that something profound is likely to occur at that age, and that gives us an opportunity to strengthen our inner awareness and resolve, our family ties and friendships, and be willing to meet change and challenge as best we can. Or, if you are a parent, to be aware that there will be a potentially life-altering situation in your child's life at a particular future time means you can help your child to be an emotionally and spiritually healthy being, ready to face and accept the numerous changes in life.

In Anna's case, she was pretty certain she wasn't born with that mole, and when she delved into the family photo albums the next week, she noticed that the mole first appeared around the age of six, when she took her first ballet lesson.

BROW BONES

control   anger   Wood   liver   green   mid 20s through early 30s

Here's the only facial feature that some of us have and some of us don't. Even those who think they have no cheekbones actually do have them. And receding chins may seem to have fallen off, but they're still there. Yet, while everyone has a frontal bone, the forehead, not everyone has a buildup of bone forming a ridge just above or along the eyebrows, the supraorbital ridge.

Men naturally have more pronounced brow ridges because they have more testosterone, which is key to the development of the brow bones and jaws. However, not all men have an obvious supraorbital brow ridge, and a few women do.

Our brow bones tell us if we have issues with control and domination. Like all the features, more is more, so the more prominent your brow bones, the more domination and control are going to be part of your day-to-day challenges.

ALWAYS CONSIDER THE **WOOD ELEMENT** ASSOCIATIONS FOR THE **BROW BONES**

characteristic	control
emotion	anger
element	Wood
organ	liver
color	green
ages	midtwenties through early thirties

Sizes and Shapes

smooth/flat brow bones	normal responses to control issues
prominent brow bones	issues with control and domination
prominent brow bones with dip in middle	ask, don't order

A former student of Traditional Chinese Medicine, Serena, told our class that her husband had **prominent brow bones** that formed two knobby ridges over each eye. But, she assured us, he was not a control freak. In fact, she worried that he gave away too much of his power to anyone who had authority over him, especially his parents. Serena made the mistake many do when learning about the brow bones and the issue of control. How you experience the issue and how you behave can take many forms. Being a control freak is just one response to having control as your issue. Another response is to be hyperalert to being controlled by another, or to be so in control of yourself that you never relax and enjoy spontaneity.

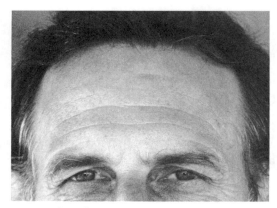

Prominent brow bones

Smooth, flat brow bones

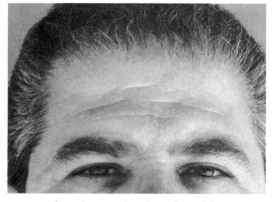

Prominent brow bones with a dip in the middle

Since men usually have the supraorbital ridge and most women don't, for each gender we determine differently whether the brow bones are prominent. A little brow bone protrusion in a man could be considered normal, while in a woman it would most likely be considered prominent.

Remember the significances of the right and left sides of the face. A more prominent brow ridge on your right side may mean that you appear to the outer world to be more controlling than you feel inside, or perhaps your mother had a formidable influence on how you relate to the issues of control and dominance. If the opposite is true, and the left side of your brow ridge is more prominent, ask yourself if you have learned to hide from the outside world your issues with control. And think about how your father influenced your feelings and behaviors around control.

My former teaching assistant had semi-**prominent brow bones with a noticeable dip in the middle,** and I was always careful to *ask* him to do anything. Even an ordinary exchange between employer and employee, such as "Remember to print out the handouts for my next class and put them in my binder, before you leave today" had to be preceded by "Would you please remember to . . ." As long as it was clear that he was not being told, but being asked, he would do anything and everything in a cheerful and helpful manner.

Several years ago, an old friend with quite **prominent brow bones** was a rising feature-film director who was determined to find the love of his life, settle down, and raise a family in a cottage by the ocean. John envisioned a future life of Hollywood premieres, coaching Little League, and being doted on by his loving wife, whom he would protect from all the cares and troubles of the outside world. Since he is quite good-looking and was quickly becoming a star in his field, he had no trouble meeting beautiful and available women on both coasts. But he seldom had more than two or three dates with any of them. He couldn't figure it out. Morning after morning he would regale our breakfast group with the grumblings of a man bemoaning the loss of an entire species—the loving and caring woman. I knew the problem from the start. John was attracted to beautiful, brilliant, successful career women. But from the moment he met them he tried to dominate them. He was not picking up the cues that these were not women who took kindly to being controlled, nor did they need to be taken care of. When I suggested to him that what he claimed he was attracted to and what he wanted out of a relationship didn't add up, he got angry. He yelled (insisting he wasn't yelling but was just impassioned), thumped the table, and did his best to convince me how wrong I was about everything regarding men, women, and love.

A mutual friend who was with us that morning called me later to marvel at my restraint. I laughed and explained that not only didn't I take John's frequent outbursts of dominance personally, I actually understood that it was his nature. John has a brow bone that is more than a ridge; it's almost a shelf hanging over his close-set, intense eyes. It's his nature to want to dominate and control every situation and person—even those he cares about and loves. That doesn't mean I liked his yelling and bullying, but I did understand he had not yet learned that his natural challenges could be tempered; that behind the yelling and control there truly was passion, he just had to learn the difference between the two feelings and the two behaviors. I sincerely believe that if John (and everyone with a pronounced brow bone) had an opportunity to recognize the challenges that this ridge warns about, he might, just might, be willing to admit that opposing opinions and ways have validity, and that he could learn from others as well as teach and preach.

So far that hasn't been the path for John. Although he did finally concede that he would be better off with a more traditional, stay-at-home kind of woman rather than the high-powered, successful executive or performer he had been pursuing. He did find her pretty quickly, and they had a beautiful storybook wedding. I wish I could say they lived happily ever after.

On a more humorous note, I once had a client from New York who had the most **pronounced brow bones** I had ever seen on a woman. Angelina was a short, plump, pretty bundle of energy who wanted to have a better relationship with her three grown children, all of whom worked together at the third-generation family café. Before I left Los Angeles I told Angelina that it would be best for me to meet the family all together, rather than one at a time. The moment my plane landed in Newark, Angelina whisked me away to the family business, where I waited for her children to join us. She cornered me, literally, in the small café, plying me with three strong espressos and some of the best pastry I have ever tasted in my life (and I've had a lot of pastry), while she recited the litany of her children's rebellions. I must have made the appropriate murmurings because she finally agreed to take me through the swinging doors into the kitchen to meet the children she adored, but who were frustrating her deeply.

I was shocked to see that her daughters were the waitress who had brought me my many fantastic treats and the cashier who had sat maybe four feet from our table, obviously hearing every word, while her mother had listed her misgivings for nearly an hour. While the daughters were shoulder to shoulder on the far side of the kitchen island, Angelina's son assured us he was paying attention while popping pastries in and out of the blasting ovens.

"Well," I began with a smile to the two women, who were behaving as though the kitchen island between us was their safeguard, "why don't you tell me what you think are the biggest challenges for your family working together?"

"I already told you," Angelina said impatiently.

"But I'd like to hear what your children have to say," I replied. "Wouldn't you?"

"I already know what they think," she said curtly. Then she added heavily, "And they're wrong."

The two young women flashed each other a knowing look, and I struggled to keep my own face impassive.

"Let's give it a try anyway," I urged.

For several seconds the four of us stood staring at each other across the island. Finally the oldest daughter stammered, "She . . . Mom doesn't really ever listen to us. About anything."

"Yes, I do."

"No, you don't. Mom, you're . . . well, you're controlling."

Angelina looked as though she had been slapped with the wet pastry bag lying on the table. I thought she might actually be speechless, for once. But then she drew herself up to her full four-foot-eleven-inch height and announced, "I am *not* controlling. I'm right." Now that that was cleared up, she turned on her crepe heel and sailed out of the kitchen.

Since that day I have taught my students that the motto of the prominent-browed person is *I'm not controlling; I'm right.* It's just such a wonderfully perfect description.

EYEBROWS

temper passion pride anger Wood liver green
early to mid 30s

In perusing my local newspaper's headlines a couple days ago, I found that a severance package, a governor's trip, a private deal, a movie star's spending spree, the police department's methods, a court nomination, and a student's hostile language all raised eyebrows. Yes, the eyebrows are the cynic's greatest tool.

Without a word, a raise or wiggle of an eyebrow can communicate volumes. My ninth-grade homeroom teacher could send ice water running through our veins with the slightest knitting of her eyebrows.

Your eyebrows keep the rain and perspiration out of your eyes, as well as the falling dust and debris.

In the world of beauty the eyebrow ranks high. Shaping, plucking, trimming, tweezing, waxing, threading, coloring, tattooing, and piercing the eyebrows is a billion-dollar business.

In the study of Mien Shiang, however, the eyebrows tell us how much passion and temper one has, as well as pride.

Along with the brow bones, the eyebrows are the facial feature most clearly likened to the Wood element. And Wood people are most influenced by their anger and drive. So it's safe to say that most—not all, but most—Wood element people have prominent eyebrows of one sort or another.

> *Your eyebrow hairs may never turn gray; if they do,*
> *it will probably be after the hairs on your head*
> *have all turned.*

As with all the features, more is more and less is less. Strong, thick, full, coarse eyebrows equal more temper as well as more passion. Softer, thinner, smaller brows indicate someone with little natural temper and few passions.

Continue to keep in mind the significance of the left and right sides of your face when doing your reading. If your right eyebrow is bushier, thicker, or coarser, you might act as though you have more of a temper than you feel deep inside. Ask yourself why you need to put on this act to the outside world. Perhaps you needed a defense mechanism as a young child? If so, examine your present life and see if you still need the world to see you as angrier, and therefore more powerful, than you truly feel.

ALWAYS CONSIDER THE **WOOD ELEMENT** ASSOCIATIONS FOR THE **EYEBROWS**

characteristics	passion, temper, pride
emotion	anger
element	Wood
organ	liver
color	green
ages	early to midthirties

The **ideal eyebrows** begin at the inner corner of the eye, peak at the outer iris, and end just beyond the outer eye corners. They should be full, but not too full, naturally well-shaped, and smooth.

With all of the above-mentioned shaping, plucking, and coloring, it's hard to tell what most people's natural eyebrows look like. I used to associate that with women, but more and more men are redesigning their brows. One trendsetting company sells human-hair eyebrows for the man who wants "a more masculine appearance."

Unless you have overplucked, shaved, or tattooed your eyebrow area, the concentration of eyebrow hairs tends to remain the same throughout life, though some do get coarser and wirier with age. The hairs that grow in the Yin Tong area (above the nose) grow nearly vertical, while the rest of the hairs are more horizontal. Men have thicker and straighter eyebrows, set level with the brow bone (the superior orbital rim); women's are thinner and curved, often curving higher than the orbital rim.

*Mona Lisa, like many of the fashionable women of
her day, shaved off her eyebrows.*

Set and Position

As the prominence of the eyebrows tells us about our anger and passion, their positioning, set, shapes, and textures all reveal varied personality traits, too.

high-set eyebrows	aloof, formal, caring, sensitive
low-set eyebrows	helpful, involved, ambitious
wide-set eyebrows	generous, common sense, insecure, good friends
close-set eyebrows	genuine, self-confident, realistic, quick to anger, resentful
connected eyebrows	angry, depressed, provoking, easily offended/insulted
eyebrows of significantly different heights	stepmother, moody, heavily socialized, overly sensitive
eyebrows down low inside	high expectations for self
eyebrows up high inside	high expectations of others

The eyebrow raise universally signals a challenge or at least a sharp questioning. Those with naturally **high-set eyebrows** have a perpetual look that seems to demand that you explain yourself. The higher the eyebrow, the more aloof and formal one appears and usually behaves.

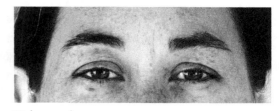

High-set eyebrows

One day my friend Tom and I crossed paths with a beautiful model who I knew slightly. I made a quick introduction and we chatted a few minutes. It was evident that Tom was a bit smitten. When we were again alone, I suggested he ask her out, since I knew she had recently become suddenly single. He looked at me as though I had suggested he kidnap the queen. "I couldn't get near her," he said to me with an exasperated wave of his hand.

"You were just very near her. And she laughed at your silly joke, too," I protested. "She liked you."

Tom thought about it, then said, "Nah, she looks too unapproachable."

"But she's obviously not. It's because her eyebrows are so high; she only looks aloof. She's actually a warm and sensitive woman."

"No. Won't work. I'd always be wondering what she's really thinking. Who she's really thinking about. You know."

Unfortunately, I did know. I'd always believed that Tom's own connected eyebrows were the evidence of why he has never had a successful long-term romance. Though I was initially frustrated that I couldn't matchmake two people whom I liked

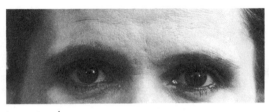
Low-set eyebrows

a lot, I eventually realized that Tom had saved both himself and the warm and beautiful model from beginning a doomed relationship. I'm still working on him to pull out a few eyebrow hairs to give himself some more room, not only between the brows, but in his romantic choices. So far he's been too stubborn to do it.

We call the **low-set eyebrow** the coaches' eyebrows because those people love to help out, but they have to *show* you exactly how to do it. Think of those Little League coaches who demonstrate to the kids exactly how to hold the bat, "just like this," and who are forever grass-stained from showing the best way to steal a base.

Not only are they helpful, but they are also very ambitious. If you are willing to do things their way, they will take you all the way to the top with them.

People whose eyebrows are **wide-set** are invariably loyal and generous friends. They have common sense and will give you solid advice, but only if you ask them.

Wide-set eyebrows

Their insecurity makes them a little shy in their romantic pursuits, though once they are in a relationship they relax their inhibitions in all aspects of their lives.

Those with **close-set eyebrows** are genuine and have a healthy dose of self-confidence. But sometimes they are so realistic that they cannot support others'

Close-set eyebrows

dreams and schemes if they are in any way fanciful. Yet it's their quick temper and resentment that brings their biggest challenges. The resentment often follows from their mounting frustration when others do not see or do things their way. When this happens, they need to step back and open their naturally bright minds and warm hearts.

If the person with the **connected eyebrows,** or **unibrow,** makes it to their midthirties without having alienated all of

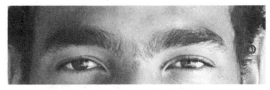

Barely connected eyebrows, lessening the challenges of the unibrow

their family and friends, they will do fine. Up until then, they have major issues with their anger and relationships. What they don't realize is that it's their own edgy, provoking nature that initiates their strife. Instead, they see themselves as being taken advantage of, insulted, and disrespected; they become the perpetually injured, retaliating victim. Luckily, as they age and mellow, they begin to take responsibility for their behavior. Plucking the middle hairs from the connected brow does help to alleviate their provocative nature. I know a couple students with connected brows who decided not to pluck those middle hairs, but instead decided to draw upon the strengths of their other natural gifts to help them be less provoking or easily offended. I've noticed that this simple acknowledgment and action has worked well for them.

Do you know anyone who is moody, overly sensitive, and ingratiating? It makes me laugh when I ask this question in corporate seminars because everyone's hand shoots

The right eyebrow is only slightly higher

right up; it seems every department has one. When I ask them to check and see if their ingratiating coworker has **eyebrows of significantly different heights,** I'm not surprised to find out that most often they do. Another trait that many of these people have is that they had stepmothers in their adolescent or teen years. Because the eyebrows represent anger, passion, and events that occur in one's twenties, and the forehead signifies the teenage years and separation from parents, I think that the different-height eyebrows, one reaching up (or back) to the teenage years and the other staying in the proper place of the early adult years, symbolize the

conflict they had in trying to separate from a parent to whom they were not truly connected. When I present this theory to those with eyebrows of radically different heights, they nearly always concur.

When the inside points of your eyebrows **dip down low,** pointing to the

Eyebrows down low inside

Eyebrows up high inside

bridge of your nose, it indicates that you have high expectations for yourself. If they point **up high inside,** you have high expectations of others. A little shaping to straighten them out might help with the stress of having high expectations of yourself or of others.

*Priests of ancient Egypt plucked not only all their
eyebrows and eyelashes, but every hair from
their bodies.*

Texture, Shape, and Length

The longer the eyebrow, the better.

The length of our eyebrows reveals how much sibling support we had in our youth, and how much support we can expect from friends and coworkers as adults. The longer the brows, the more support.

An eyebrow that reaches to the outer corner of the eye is considered an average eyebrow. The eyebrow that does not reach the outer corner of the eye would be a short eyebrow, and one that extends beyond is a long eyebrow.

long eyebrows	good sibling support, sensitive, dedicated, loves beauty
short eyebrows	poor sibling support, sensitive, orderly, doesn't ask for help
full (thick) eyebrows	anger, passion, courageous, generous to loved ones, likes action
bushy eyebrows	courageous, anger, passion, stubborn, argumentative, generous
bushy, thick, messy eyebrows	angry, violent
sparse to nonexistent eyebrows	helpful, indirect, indecisive, fear of being wrong
thin eyebrows	shy, timid, quiet, scattered
eyebrows that connect to hairline	intelligent, high achiever

Long eyebrows

Long eyebrows, those that extend at least to the outer corner of the eye or longer, not only indicate that you have had good sibling support, but that you are dedicated to your loved ones. The longer the brows, the more sensitive you are to discord among your family and friends. A little beauty in your life will always pick up your spirits.

Even though they can have lots of friends, those with **short eyebrows** don't have many true friends. I think that because they didn't have sibling support when they were young, they haven't learned to bond or to trust that others are there for them. They are restless, easily hurt, and have a sense of loneliness even when in good relationships. Since they were self-sufficient children, they have trouble asking for help

Short eyebrows

and therefore are not the best team players. A man with short eyebrows told me recently that he did not have sibling support because he didn't allow his brothers and sister to support him. He had decided as a youngster that his role in the family was the caretaker. Because he wanted so badly to live up to his father's strict expectations, he did not want to risk appearing weak by accepting help from anyone. He grew up to be a success, even in his father's eyes, but he yearns for a more equal relationship with his adult siblings. I'm waiting to see if his short eyebrows will lengthen if he does achieve that.

It's great to have someone close to you with **full,** as in **thick, eyebrows** as they are courageous and generous to those they care deeply about. Since they have such strong emotions and crave lots of action, they seldom hesitate to defend what they

Full, thick eyebrows

believe is theirs, whether family, friends, territory, or country. Eyebrows most represent the Wood personality traits, and anger is the emotion that challenges them the most. If you have full, thick eyebrows and your anger often overwhelms you, use your love of action to find a way to channel it into constructive passion.

If you have **bushy eyebrows** (a little shaggy as well as full), you have the same

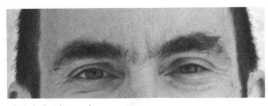
Slightly bushy eyebrows

traits as those with full, thick eyebrows. You have an additional challenge of stubbornness, especially when you are embroiled in one of those lively debates you love so much. What you might view as a passionate exchange, others might interpret as an intense argument. Take a deep breath; maybe even bite your tongue. Let your natural generosity be your stronger suit when things get overheated.

People with **thick, bushy, and messy eyebrows that are wild and unkempt** look angry and they generally are, going into unprovoked rages that can easily lead to violence. Cut them a wide swath.

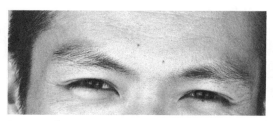

Sparse eyebrows

Indirect, indecisive people who have a fear of being wrong often have **sparse or naturally nonexistent eyebrows.** I have a friend who has such faint, delicate eyebrows that they seem nonexistent, and when I first knew him, I thought that he was one of the few people who didn't fit the profile.

He is generous and caring, the kind of friend who is sincerely interested in your well-being and stands up for you even before you ask for his support. But over the years it has become apparent that he doesn't know how to ask for what he needs. He frequently coaxes and nudges me into doing things for him that I hadn't wanted to do, yet he is uncannily subtle about it; it's not until later that I realize I've been manipulated.

Though he is truly generous, he regularly hints that he never receives as much as he gives out. I've realized that he backs up all of his statements with tons of research, not because he is the avid researcher that he claims to be, but because he is scared of being wrong. Maybe if he didn't have such sparse, hard-to-see eyebrows, I might be more annoyed with him. But knowing that this is one of his life's challenges endears him to me. Because, even though those traits sound so unappealing on the written page, in life my friend is just that, my friend. Someone who, like all of us, has his struggles, but his good points—a generous heart and soul make it all worthwhile.

It's interesting to note that some people who are fair-skinned with white-blond hair appear to have little or no eyebrows, but on close examination there are more hairs and texture than is apparent at first glance. A good reminder not to make Mien Shiang conclusions from afar.

Shy, timid, quiet people often have

Thin eyebrows

naturally delicate, **thin eyebrows.** They don't trust their instincts and end up scattering their energies by beginning more projects than they can finish. Keep that in mind when you shape your eyebrows.

I have seldom seen eyebrows that **connect to the hairline,** but when I visited my friend in his laboratory at Caltech, I saw three people in one afternoon with those eyebrows. My friend confirmed my suspicion that each of them was extremely intelligent and a high achiever. He claimed he expected at least two of the three to eventually win international accolades for their brilliance.

Markings on the Eyebrows

REMINDER ABOUT FACIAL MARKINGS

Markings such as scars, lines, and some discolorations are acquired, while others, such as moles and birthmarks, can be inherited.

Markings on the left or right sides of the face reveal father's or mother's influence as well as your own inner or outer personality and behavior.

Markings on the eyebrows reveal events that have happened, or are likely to happen, in your early to midthirties. Because the eyebrows are the facial features most associated with Wood and anger, markings on the brows directly affect the expression of that emotion. A few years ago, I was visiting a client at her home in Bel Air, California. Caroline pleaded with me to speak to her fifteen-year-old daughter, who had recently, against her mother's wishes, pierced her right eyebrow. The last thing I wanted was to get in the middle of a family argument, but Tracy, the daughter, thought it might be interesting to have a little fun with me and my "hocus-pocus." I took a deep breath and joined Tracy in the family media room.

Tracy was a beautiful, friendly girl, who told me that a few of her friends had multiple ear piercings, and a couple had delicate nose studs, but no one in her circle had been so "out there" as she was with her eyebrow ring. Tracy did well in school and had good friends, a great boyfriend, and never got in trouble until "the piercing thing."

"Oh, yeah," she said as if just remembering, "I also did it because I thought it would drive my mom nuts."

"Seems to have worked," I said. "Any reasons other than you're fifteen?"

Tracy shrugged as though a bit embarrassed. "My mom worries about everything. It's like I can't breathe, she's so suffocating. I just thought I'd give her something real to worry about for a change. But I still think it's kind of cool, the 'brow ring."

"Cool counts for a lot," I agreed. "This might sound odd, Tracy, but since you pierced your eyebrow, have you noticed that you're angrier than usual?"

Tracy looked surprised and then narrowed her eyes at me. "My mom told you that, right?"

"Honest, she didn't. Have you?"

"All the time in school. I never get in trouble and lately I'm so pissed off with my teachers, and I know I'm rude, but I can't help it. It's not like me. And I'm arguing with Jared, my boyfriend, all the time over nothing. And you can imagine what it's been like with my mother." Suddenly she looked so miserable.

"Tracy, I know you think Mien Shiang, face reading, is hocus-pocus, but I might be able to help you."

"I don't really think it is," she said, rolling her eyes. "It was just to annoy my mother."

So I told her about the different facial features representing specific emotions and behavioral traits, especially about eyebrows and anger. "As crazy as this may sound, I believe that your eyebrow piercing has stimulated your anger. And it's on the right side of your face, which represents your outer behavior—and your mother's influence! Would you be willing to try an experiment? You don't even have to tell your mom; it can be just between you and me."

Tracy agreed to remove her eyebrow ring when she went to class for the entire next week, and when she went out with Jared or talked with him on the phone. (This was before constant e-mailing and text messaging, so we didn't have to factor that into our experiment.) She wasn't ready to "give in" to her mother, so she was going to wear the eyebrow ring at home.

She promised to let me know at the end of the week if she noticed any difference with her anger issues.

"I don't believe this," she said when she called to report that she had had a fantastic week getting along with everyone, just as she used to.

"How about with your mom?"

"Well"—she hesitated—"maybe now I'll sound crazy to you. I wore the 'brow ring all week at home, but I didn't argue with my mom nearly as much as I had been. But I felt like I was standing up to her better than I usually do. Does that make sense?"

"Absolutely. The other side of anger is passion. Maybe since you're not so angry with your teachers and boyfriend, you've subconsciously decided you also want to get along better with your mother. Also, it's possible that instead of your eyebrow ring provoking your anger all the time, it's now stimulating your passion to live your own life and trust your own instincts. That would naturally make you feel less angry with your mother."

Tracy was pleased with our experiment and promised to keep me posted about any changes. That reminded me to tell her that she had pierced the age area for thirty-three, so there was a possibility that by stimulating that area now she might have given herself reason to be especially alert to any life-changing events when she reached thirty-three. It's great to have some forewarning of change so that we are prepared to keep ourselves healthy and balanced in all ways.

YIN TONG

relationship to father anger Wood liver green late 20s and early 30s

The Yin Tong is the area above the nose and between the eyebrows. This little section of your face speaks volumes about your relationship to your father (or your father figure) in your youth and your ability to express anger in a healthy way. Since the Yin Tong is so revealing about our anger issues, it is obviously a Wood element area.

ALWAYS CONSIDER THE **WOOD ELEMENT** ASSOCIATIONS FOR THE **YIN TONG**

characteristic	relationship to father
emotion	anger
element	Wood
organ	liver
color	green
ages	late twenties and early thirties

Suspended Needles

The vertical lines in the Yin Tong that we commonly refer to as frown lines are in the language of Mien Shiang called **Estrangement from Father Lines** or **Suspended Needles.** These lines, or Needles, indicate the inability to express anger, or to express it appropriately, because of not having been allowed to *feel* anger as a child. One person in the family, usually the father, assumed the role of the Keeper of Anger. He alone was allowed to be angry, and anyone else, especially his child, would have to sublimate this emotion. The child grows up feeling that he has had the anger beaten out of him whether it's physically, emotionally, spiritually, or all three.

We see these lines most often on Wood people who had a Wood parent with their own unresolved and intense issues with anger, but all elemental types can have them.

If you have never been allowed to express your anger, you haven't learned to stand up for yourself either. When you finally do give it a try, you probably won't be very good at it at first. As we have said earlier, anger is a complex emotion, and in a healthy world our parents and teachers help us learn its suitable expression. When you haven't had that guidance, you tend to make mistakes.

Once you start to communicate your anger and assert yourself, even if you are faltering or act inappropriately sometimes, you will possibly get a second, fainter line in

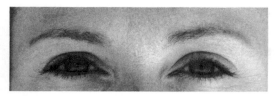

No lines in the Yin Tong

One line in the Yin Tong

Two lines in the Yin Tong

Three lines in the Yin Tong

the Yin Tong area. Celebrate that line as a mark of moving forward in a healthier way. In time you will find that you are more comfortable with yourself and with expressing your true feelings. That's when a third line will appear, reminding you of your great accomplishment.

You can determine the severity of the estrangement from the father and the degree of difficulty regarding expressing anger by the depth and length of the Suspended Needle. If the line is quite deep and long, we upgrade it to a Suspended Sword, and when it is very deep, long, and perhaps jagged, we refer to it as a Suspended Dagger.

Discoloration that appears in the Yin Tong area is significant, too. Several times I have noticed a small brown or greenish patch suddenly appear between my eyebrows. Since the color green (and greenish brown) is the Wood element color, and the area itself has significant Wood element characteristics, the discoloration often confirms to me that I am repressing anger or backing off from my power, and that I need to resolve the issue. More than once I have noticed a green discoloration in my Yin Tong when I'm not even conscious of being angry, and it has prompted me to question my true feelings regarding an event or situation. It's an invaluable indicator for me to take a look at what is going on in my life, and to set things right—especially because I tend to avoid confrontation and angry feelings.

Red markings, such as a little pimple or a dry, scaly patch, indicate more of a conscious inflamed anger that you are not dealing with, rather than a deep, repressed one that you are not aware of. As when you deal with your repressed anger, you will see that as soon as you have resolved the disturbing angry feelings, the redness also disappears quickly.

With patience and sincerity we can all learn the healthy expression of all our emotions and freely experience our joy and passion for life.

EYES

receptivity/passion Wood/Fire green/red mid 30s to early 40s

You don't have to be a face reader to learn plenty about people simply by looking into their eyes. In a flash you can tell if they are happy, sad, scared, or confused. We know if someone is suspicious or calculating when they narrow their eyes at us, or that they are happy to see us when those eyes open wide and shine.

The emotions of the eyes are Fire.
The function of the eyes is Wood.

Cicero (106–43 BC) said, "The face is a picture of the mind as the eyes are its interpreter," the forerunner to the more familiar phrase "The eyes are the mirror to the soul."

In the Taoist Five Element theory, the Shen, your spirit, which is much like your soul, resides in your heart. Your eyes reflect the state of your Shen; the clearer they are and the more sparkle they have, the healthier your Shen. The more open your eyes are—the more shine, sparkle, warmth, and awareness—the more you take in emotionally and spiritually from the outer world, and you will give out much love from your heart and soul (your Shen) to others and to your environment. If your eyes are closed and guarded, the less you will take in and give out since you are too intent on protecting your heart.

In Mien Shiang we read the eyes for two different purposes, each ruled by a different element. One is, as we just mentioned, to determine the health and state of the emotions and the Shen, and this is governed by the element Fire.

The second reason we analyze the eyes is to ascertain intelligence and the basic health of the eyes—their vision and function—and this is governed by the element Wood.

Therefore, the state of your Shen and the emotions that are expressed through your eyes are analyzed as Fire issues, and we analyze your intelligence and the function of your eyes, such as being nearsighted, farsighted, or having cataracts or eye irritations, as Wood conditions.

ALWAYS CONSIDER THE **FIRE ELEMENT** ASSOCIATIONS FOR THE **EYES**

characteristic	receptivity/Shen
emotion	joy
element	Fire
organ	heart
color	red
ages	midthirties to early forties

as well as . . .

characteristics	intelligence, health, vision, function
emotion	anger
element	Wood
organ	liver
color	green
ages	midthirties to early forties

Size and Shape

wide-open eyes	receptive, absorbent, big emotions
narrower eyes	perceptive, watchful, wary, analytical
nearsighted	detail-oriented
farsighted	see the big picture
large eyes	intelligent, imaginative, likes attention
large, bright eyes	high-spirited
large, very bright eyes	high-spirited, aggressive
large, soft eyes	idealistic dreamer
large, very soft eyes	a dreamer, romantically unrealistic
very large eyes	scattered, difficulty communicating
small eyes	curious, impatient, insecure about love
very small eyes	ambitious, self-referential, materialistic
round eyes	bright, alert, happy, caring, attractive
almond eyes	sensual, self-discipline

As you might assume, the more **wide-open** your eyes are, the more you take in and give out. You are receptive, absorbent, and tend to have big emotions. The **narrower** your eyes, the more perceptive, watchful, wary, and analytical you are.

Though these eyes are not big, they are wide-open, taking in and giving out energy.

Narrow eyes

Ideal eyes are fully open, clear as a lake, with a slight shine and good vision.

Vision is congenital, or inherited. If you inherited **nearsightedness,** you also inherited its trait of being detail-oriented. Your inheritance of **farsightedness** includes your ability to see the big picture.

Large eyes

Considering our eyes reveal the state of our Shen, **large eyes** reflect the gift of a healthier emotional and spiritual balance, as well as intelligence, imagination, and a desire for attention.

This is a good time to reiterate the meaning of gifts and challenges. If your eyes are not large, it does not mean that you do not have a healthy emotional and spiritual balance, or that you lack intelligence, imagination, or a desire for attention. It means that those who do have large eyes have to put in a little less effort in those areas than the rest of us. As we've noted before, working for something often makes it more rewarding.

If those **large eyes are also bright,** these people have the same traits, but they are more high-spirited. If those large eyes are **very bright,** that high-spirited energy can become a bit too aggressive, especially when it comes to getting needs met.

Large and bright eyes

Large and soft eyes

Large and soft eyes belong to idealistic dreamers willing to fight for their dreams. **Large eyes that are very soft** indicate the dreamer who loses himself in unrealistic fantasies, especially romantic ones. He is smart in most other aspects of life, but this trait can be his undoing.

People with **very large eyes** have scattered thoughts and feelings, making it hard for them to communicate clearly. They just take in and give out too much of their emotions and spirit to be able to focus.

Since those with **small eyes** are more conservative with their emotions, whether they give them out or take them in, they are naturally more self-attentive and self-

Small eyes

aware. When they are confronted with the big emotions of others, they become impatient with what they see as their over-the-top antics. Until they are reassured and feel safe, they are hesitant to connect on a deep emotional and spiritual level. Though they do have a curious nature, it is within their own small circle of interests.

Those with **very small eyes** are self-centered to the point of being selfish, even with loved ones. Their materialism and ambition bring them success in business, but not in romance and friendship. The good part is that they don't care, as long as they have their possessions and are in control.

Round eyes

The **rounder** your eyes, the happier you are. And why not? You are bright, alert, enterprising, caring, and sexually attractive. Those who have **almond-shaped eyes** have enough self-discipline not to get carried away by their innate sensuality. Others, however, are easily carried away by their alluring nature.

Almond eyes

Set and Positioning

wide-set eyes	big picture, open, expectations, memory, naïve, moody
close-set eyes	focused, analytical, social, successful, irritable, ego
deep-set eyes	inward, contemplative, romantic, critical, late bloomers
bulging or protruding eyes	"out there," ego, exhibitionists, imagination, temper
eyes with lower inside corner (cat's eyes)	beauty, curious, mercurial, magnetic, playfully seductive
eyes with downward slanting/ higher inside corner	self-sacrificing, trusting, need friends and family

If you have **wide-set eyes,** you can see the big picture of any situation, you are blessed with a good memory, and you're open to all sorts of new ideas and events, es-

Wide-set eyes

pecially romantic ones. Your naïveté can add to your charms or get you in trouble; it all depends on keeping your moodiness under control. You have exceptionally high expectations for yourself, but you can lack the "oomph" to carry through on many of those big ambitions. Be kind to yourself. Give yourself more realistic goals and parameters, and you can soar.

I am fascinated by the contrasts of some of my friends with **close-set eyes.** They are social, entertaining, and great hosts with extended circles of friends, mostly asso-

Close-set eyes

ciated with their successful business enterprises. Their gift of focus, particularly with minute details, and their natural analytical abilities and strong egos enable them to be powerful leaders with innovative platforms. Yet, when they are challenged or when they don't get their way, I've seen them become unduly irritable and narrow-minded, even combative. Once their argumentative stance and position has been made clear, they can quickly move on and recapture their former happy-host persona. They are often bewildered as to why others are "holding on, and making a big deal of it. It's over! Let's have some fun."

Deep-set eyes were called bedroom eyes in our great-grandparents' generation. These inward, contemplative people are romantics who reveal only little bits of them-

Deep-set eyes

selves to their partners, creating an aura of mystery. They attract many lovers, but because they can be so critical and play the push-pull game in romance, their affairs are short-lived. By the time they reach their mid-thirties, they are ready to settle down with one mate. They are also late bloomers in their careers, but that's not surprising given how much time and energy they devote to romance in their youth.

It is either entertaining or embarrassing to be related to the person with the **bulging or protruding eyes.** They are "out there" exhibitionists, unable or unwilling to temper their actions or words. Even after they have caused a scandal or major chaos, their large egos, strong wills, and lively imaginations stop them from keeping their promises to rein in their behavior. There's a better chance that they will fly into a rage and accuse you of manipulating them. Barbara Bush fits the physical description, and she did have of history of making outrageous statements long before her comments regarding the displaced Hurricane Katrina victims who had been shuttled to the Houston arena.

Eyes with lower inside corners are considered by many cultures to represent ideal physical beauty. They are also called cat's eyes, and the disposition seems to fit: curious, magnetic, and playfully seductive, with a mercurial temperament.

"Cat's eyes" with lower inside corners

The Taoists say that you were born to be sad if you have downward-slanting eyes with **higher inside corners.** This sadness is a blessing for others, though, since it relates to your reacting to the injustices of the world. You have an innate need to right those ills and could devote your life doing so. Your desire to be connected to family or your family of friends can lead you to be too self-sacrificing and trusting.

Eyes with higher inside corners

And if you get hurt too often, you will withdraw and seek an even-tempered life. Be careful not to cut yourself off from your own needs and dreams for the sake of others or to avoid being hurt.

Markings Around the Eyes

REMINDER ABOUT FACIAL MARKINGS

Markings such as scars, lines, and some discolorations are acquired, while others, such as moles and birthmarks, can be inherited.

Markings on the left or right sides of the face reveal father's or mother's influence as well as your own inner or outer personality and behavior.

Just as our eyes reveal much about our present emotions, the markings around our eyes divulge much about our past and how we have responded to grief, broken hearts, sadness, physical pain, and even our issues with fidelity.

lines of lost love	deep heartbreak
sadness lines	profound sadness
physical pain lines	chronic pain
grief lines	unresolved grief
puffy under eyes/Unshed Tears	inability to shed tears of past sadness

The delicate area right under the eyes is a canvas for the lines that reveal our emotional upheavals. Straight lines (not curving, jagged, or broken, but very straight) that

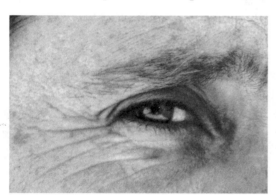

Lines of lost love

begin under the eyes nearer to the inside eye corner and extend straight toward the outside eye corners or beyond are called **lines of lost love,** resulting from devastating heartbreak. Most often these lines are found on the Fire person who sank into the depths of despair after losing a great love and has never completely resolved her heartache. Unfortunately nearly everyone can identify with the pain of heartbreak, but few have experienced the despair and hopelessness that the person with the lines of lost love felt.

The little lines that fan out from the outer corners of the eyes frequently belong to the lucky person who laughs a lot and deeply, so that their whole face lifts and crinkles in laughter. Sometimes those fanned lines are actually **sadness lines,** coming from quite a different facial expression and emotion. Pretend you are about to audition for the role of a tragically sad character. How could you show that on your face, other than with downcast eyes and slack mouth and jaw? Imagine how painful it is to feel profoundly sad. As you begin to feel that pain, do you notice you begin to wince, scrunching your upper cheeks around the outer corners of your eyes? That feeling, leading to that wincing, results in sadness lines that ironically resemble their opposite, the laugh lines. We've all been in a situation of not knowing whether to laugh or cry; this is one time it wouldn't make a difference to the outcome of the facial lines.

Those who have **chronic physical pain** also wince and tighten their faces, but it's less on the cheeks and more around the eyes, especially the outer corners, which they tighten inward as though trying to pull in their pain. Those lines begin at the outside corners and extend at an angle toward the nose (though not that far).

Grief lines begin anywhere under the eye and go downward in a straight line.

Any of the elemental personality types can have grief lines since we all experience deep grief, but we see them mostly on Metal people, even those who have not experienced loss of loved ones. Their grief lines represent their own ongoing sense of loss.

Another common condition we see under the eyes is what we call **Unshed Tears.** It is a chronic puffiness not caused by allergies or sleepiness, but literally by the inability to shed the tears of past sadness. Once you release the pain by releasing the tears, the puffiness disappears, even if you have had it for years. Many of my clients who have Unshed Tears tell me that they don't have time to cry, or they're afraid that if they do, they'll never stop. If that is your problem, too, then I suggest you make a date with yourself to have a good heartfelt cry. Choose a weekend evening when you can be alone and have nothing planned for the next morning, and do whatever is necessary to get you in the mood. Light candles, listen to sappy music, rent a tearjerker movie. Then sit quietly with your feelings and your sad memories, and let the tears flow. It's from the hard times that we most often learn our life lessons and grow, but only if we feel our feelings. Don't push down the hurts and tears; it only closes off your heart to future joy.

Unshed Tears

Marks of Infidelity

The ancient Taoists claimed that a mole or crosshatched lines at the outer corner of the eyes are marks of infidelity.

I am generally reluctant to bring up these markings because they tend to scare people. So let me use this opportunity to once again remind you that just because we have certain markings, it does not mean we are doomed, nor does it mean that we get a free ride. They are there to remind us of our specific innate gifts and challenges. They don't tell us how or if we will respond to them, only that we have them.

Therefore, if you have marks of infidelity, all you know is that this issue will be a challenge in your life. The challenge could be a struggle with your own faithfulness, or a struggle with your mate's loyalty, or even with the philosophical concept of fidelity.

I had clients, a couple, and both had marks of infidelity. Each was adamant about the rules of faithfulness, and there were no gray areas or doubts about the repercussions. They were a loving, respectful couple who gave each other plenty of room in their relationship because of their mutual clarity and trust.

Years ago I was having dinner at a cozy restaurant in Sonoma, California, preparing my final notes for a Valentine's weekend workshop I was presenting called "Mien Shiang and the Look of Love." My waitress, an attractive woman in her early forties, glanced down at one of my workshop handouts on the marks of infidelity that had two drawings of eyes and the markings. "My husband has those lines," she said, pointing to the crosshatched lines at an outer eye corner. "We just got married last month. Is he going to cheat on me?" she asked me with a little worry in her eyes.

I gave her the quick explanation about our gifts and challenges, and told her that how we each respond to them is unique and often surprising. "All you know is that he has a challenge. It may be that this challenge has made him stronger and more responsible about fidelity. Why don't you ask him?" I suggested.

She hesitated, then confided, "We were engaged twenty years ago, but we broke up because he was unfaithful. We met again last year and he seems like a changed man; he says he is. We have a lot of fun, and I do love him." I left the restaurant happy to hear about the romantic ending to her love story.

About six months later I was back in Sonoma for another workshop. Walking by a coffee shop, I was surprised to hear someone call my name. I turned and saw the waitress from my previous trip.

"I just had to tell you," she said, running up to me and catching her breath. "We're getting a divorce. He was still cheating!"

"Oh, I'm so sorry," I said.

"Me, too, but I'd rather be free again and have a chance to meet someone who's right for me. Any clues on my face as to why I've been picking the wrong men?"

I didn't need to study her face, since I remembered from our last meeting certain of her facial characteristics that had stood out to me. "I see by the way your ears come away from your head that you have a tendency to hear only what you want to hear," I said gently, so she would hear what I was saying.

"It's true," she said with a sigh. "There were lots of clues, but I didn't want to hear them. Am I hopeless?"

"Not with those jaws; you've got great determination. Use it to find the truth, and real love."

I think of her often and wonder if she has found the love she was looking for. I hope so.

CHEEKS

confidence grief Metal lungs white mid 40s and late 50s

You are cheeky if you are considered bold, rude, sassy, mischievous, or defiant. To pull off any of those attitudes, you need a good amount of confidence. The fuller your cheeks, the more energy and confidence you have. Or perhaps we could say, the cheekier you are, the more confident you are.

ALWAYS CONSIDER THE **METAL ELEMENT** ASSOCIATIONS FOR THE **CHEEKS**

characteristic	confidence
emotion	grief
element	Metal
organ	lungs
color	white
ages	mid forties and late fifties

Size and Shape

full, fleshy cheeks	confidence, sensual, vivacious, practical, enjoys life
round, high (upper) cheeks (apple)	confidence, generous, courageous, strong-willed, success-driven
curved cheeks	contemplative, communicative, interesting experiences
hollow or indented cheeks	stress, lack of "something"
thin, hollow cheeks	nervous, perfectionist, seek peace
wrinkled, thin, sagging cheeks	one who suffers, no enjoyment
flat cheeks	levelheaded, avoids personal conflict, shaky confidence, moody

Full, fleshy cheeks mean you are confident, sensual, vivacious, practical, and you enjoy life. A student once challenged the description, saying it didn't make sense:

Full, fleshy cheeks

Round, high cheeks

You couldn't be sensual, vivacious, and practical. What about Santa Claus? I asked. The class erupted in laughter, thinking I had just lost my own argument.

We know *sensual* can refer to desires and appetites of the body. Well, one look at Santa and you know he surely has those. Who can be more vivacious than a jolly old man in a bright red suit who secretly visits every country, every town, every child in the world, in one night, to leave presents, ho-ho-hoing the whole time? And practical? This man has to read every letter, determine the best present for each child, oversee his staff of elves, keep his reindeer fed and healthy and happy, make sure the sleigh is packed evenly, remember where each child lives, and make his entrance and getaway undetected. As far as I'm concerned, only a sensual, vivacious, *and* practical person could carry this off not once, but year after year.

Those who have **round, high upper cheeks** don't stay home alone much. Their confident, generous, courageous, and strong-willed personalities put them in demand socially and in business. They are driven by success and love to be challenged in their careers. But they aren't all work and no play; no one likes a practical joke—especially on themselves—as much as they do. Women with these cheeks are good with managing the stresses of home life and career, but if one of the two suffers periodically, I'd bet on the home life.

Especially contemplative, communicative people tend to have cheeks that are

curved, no matter the size of the cheeks. I wish every judge sitting in a courtroom worldwide would have these cheeks.

Hollow (or indented) cheeks indicate stress in the body or emotions, especially related to overwork. I see many hollow cheeks when my university students are in the middle of exam weeks, and frequently when I conduct corporate workshops. It seems that businesses are forever operating on deadlines that are nearly impossible for their employees to meet without becoming overstressed.

If you were born with hollow cheeks, then you either experienced physical or emotional stress in the womb, or you may have inherited this trait from either of your parents' lineage.

Curved cheeks

People with hollow cheeks often complain of feeling that they are lacking "something," but they're not sure what. I believe, of course, what they are experiencing is the lack of innate confidence. But if you have never felt it, perhaps it is difficult to express just what "it" is. If you know someone with this trait, remind them frequently of their strengths and gifts. Be generous and sincere in your praise and their confidence will grow. I'm confident of it.

Every once in a while you will see distinctly **thin and hollow cheeks.** These troubled souls have a nervous, restless temperament, forever seeking inner peace, seldom finding it. Thin, hollow, fragile-looking cheeks can be the sign of the mad artists, perfectionists never satisfied with their own, often extraordinary, achievements. Vincent van Gogh sadly fit this description to perfection, which you can plainly see in most of his self-portraits.

Some people have absolutely no enjoyment in life and seem to have made a commitment to suffering. When you see **wrinkled, thin, and sagging cheeks,** you can be pretty sure you have met one of these cheerless creatures. They are frustrating to know because you feel powerless to help them, and therefore any relationship with them leaves you exhausted, even on a good day. Until they come to terms with their deeply felt, repressed anger, they will remain a challenge to themselves and to you.

People who are predominately Wood element often have **flat cheeks,** which may be nature's way of keeping them agreeable. Since the cheeks represent confidence, and the Wood person has so many prominent features that signify strengths such as anger and passion, control and determination, perhaps it's good that they question their self-confidence, if only to create balance. My good friend Jack has flat cheeks on what I call his quintessential Wood face: rectangular shape, prominent brow bones and eyebrows, piercing eyes, and a strong, determined jawline, giving him all the assurance anyone would need. Yet, sometimes when he is tired or vulnerable, I notice his confidence can easily be shaken. But he is able to pull on the strengths of his other gifts and move forward pretty quickly. I like to tell him that if he had well-developed cheeks in addition to his other self-assured traits, he'd be insufferable. He'll just glare at me, then a bit of a smile will finally tug at the corners of his mouth. Eventually.

Those other non-Wood-element people who have flat cheeks are levelheaded with a solemn demeanor. They make undemanding bosses and coworkers because they avoid conflict. Generosity comes easily, but sometimes they can give away the store when much less would be just fine. When success comes, it is often by chance or it is granted to them as a reward for their hard work or talents, not because they have campaigned for it. They are driven by their dreams and goals, not their ambitions.

All those with flat cheeks, Wood types included, are moody. It's hard for them to communicate, even to those they love deeply, when the shroud of moodiness envelops them. They will isolate themselves, alienating and frustrating their family and friends. This behavior is especially hard on their relationships because they accept their moodiness and resent anyone who attempts to "help" them recover from it.

Middle and Lower Cheeks

The area just below the apple of the cheeks, next to the mouth, is called the lower cheek, and right next to it is the middle cheek; each area has traits associated with it that differ from those of the cheeks and cheekbones.

The old Taoist monks called the **lower cheeks,** right next to the corners of the mouth, the **moneybags.** If you are going to get rich or keep the money you already have, you need nice plump lower cheeks—or moneybags. That plumpness means you are healthy, and you have enough reserve energy to keep going when things get tough physically, emotionally, or spiritually. When you are exhausted or ill, you have no reserves, will not be able to make money, and will probably have to dip into your savings to keep going. When you don't have any reserves, your moneybags sag, giving you a jowly look. That's when you need to add fats to your diet, and other rich pleasures for your emotions and spirits. But be careful of overdoing. An excess of food and other nurturing pleasures won't add to your reserves, but instead it will weigh you down physically, emotionally, and spiritually, and your moneybags will have a lumpy, mottled texture, or what the monks call mutton-fat jade. Not a pleasant image, either way.

The monks also called the **middle cheeks** the **Breath of Life** area because it shows whether we have the desire for life. When we are in the last stages of severe illness, the middle cheeks often become hollowed and dark, showing that we have lost

our desire for this life and are preparing to enter the next transition. Suicidal people frequently have a hollowed Breath of Life area, too. When their depression lessens, the middle cheeks once again fill out.

The middle cheeks are an important indicator as to whether your lungs are in good shape, if you have enough air. When we are racing in our busy lives, we often forget to breathe correctly. We take in the breath and then hold it or breathe shallowly. Remember to slow down, breathe in, and breathe out. You will be healthier, and you won't have those drawn middle cheeks. You have probably noticed that many smokers have sunken middle cheeks from years of inhaling deeply and not exhaling fully. It is proof that they are not getting enough air into their lungs and are poisoning themselves as well.

Full middle cheeks, in the Breath of Life area, indicating a strong desire to live a full life. The dimples show joy.

Markings on the Cheeks

REMINDER ABOUT FACIAL MARKINGS

Markings such as scars, lines, and some discolorations are acquired, while others, such as moles and birthmarks, can be inherited.

Markings on the left or right sides of the face reveal father's or mother's influence as well as your own inner or outer personality and behavior.

grief lines	unresolved grief
smile lines	too much work
dimples	sensual, easygoing, inconsistent

Just like the vertical lines under the eyes, the vertical cheek lines are also called **grief lines** and represent inherited, unresolved, or chronic grief. A deep grief line only on the left cheek often indicates someone who takes on the grief of others, besides their own ongoing feelings of sorrow.

When we smile, our cheeks usually wrinkle a little. If those **smile lines** at the corners of the mouth are still present at rest, after the smile has ended, it indicates

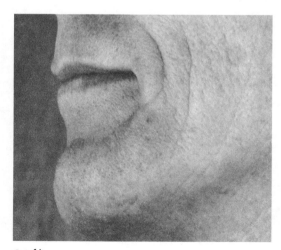

Grief lines

Smile lines

someone with a big work ethic. Too big. These people work hard at everything, including having fun and being happy. It's hard to change this behavior since they are used to being praised and rewarded for their overwork and have begun to identify themselves by what they do rather than what they feel.

Everyone loves **dimples;** they're just so appealing. Have there ever been more adorable dimples than those on little Shirley Temple's cherub cheeks? The Taoist personality traits for dimples are sensuality, an easygoing attitude, and an inconsistent or fickle nature, especially when it comes to romance. These people just have so many admirers to choose from. Once they do make their decision, though, they have romantic, long-term relationships. I wonder if these qualities fit the adult Ms. Temple, a personable, bright former U.S. diplomat who was married for many years to the same man. I have noticed that these traits do fit most charmers I've met with dimples.

A beautiful dimple

CHEEKBONES

authority grief Metal lungs white mid 40s and late 50s

The ancient Taoists said that the cheekbones are the "framers of the face" because they determine the shape of the Valleys (the soft, fleshy parts) of the face. (An interesting note: We said earlier in this book that the body and face are generally similar in shape and proportion. That would mean that most people who have big or prominent cheekbones also have prominent shoulders. Start looking and see if this fits.)

characteristic	authority
emotion	grief
element	Metal
organ	lungs
color	white
ages	midforties and late fifties

Set, Size, and Shape

prominent/high cheekbones	authority, pride, strong-willed, dynamic, independent, ambitious, ideal love
angled-down cheekbones	love to travel, bold, adventurous
very large cheekbones	authoritative, proud, assured
angular, sharp cheekbones	quick, astute, decisive, efficient, sharp
flat cheekbones	compassionate, resists authority
cheekbones set closer to nose	announces authority, mentor, generous
cheekbones set closer to ears	no warning, strong bosses, fair and generous

The more **prominent (high and developed) your cheekbones** the more natural authority you possess. You are dynamic, ambitious, persistent, independent, and strong-willed in all aspects. Since you are so competent and have a great sense of pride, be careful you don't become obstinate or vain in your pursuits. Your biggest challenge in all relationships is that you have such high ideals in life and love, and you don't want to settle for less than your ideal. Be careful not to demand the unattainable; you will only set yourself up to be alone and lonely. Accept and forgive yourself for not being perfect, and extend the same to those you care about. Remember, your high standards are simply one of your natural challenges in life. Use your gift of persistence and determination to see the humor and compassion in your imperfections. You are much more lovable than you can imagine, especially when you think so, too! Give it a try.

Once on a long flight from Los Angeles to Italy, we experienced bumpy weather over the Atlantic. I noticed that when certain flight attendants hurried up and down the aisles telling us to put up our tray tables, they were obeyed without hesitation. But other attendants, using the same words and sense of urgency, were often ignored. I had an idea why this was and decided that when things calmed down I would take a good look at all the attendants' faces to see if I was right. Sure enough, the attendants whose orders were obeyed all had prominent and high cheekbones, and the others who had been ignored had lower or flatter cheekbones. On your next interminable wait in an airport lobby, look around at the myriad of flight attendants and pilots scurrying through the terminal and see if you don't spot an excess of prominent cheekbones, as well as prominent cheekbones that are **angled down,** slanting toward the nose—a trait belonging to those who are bold, adventurous, and love to travel.

Authoritative, even prideful people almost always have **very large cheekbones.** If you have beautiful, large cheekbones, you're fortunate to have such a valuable gift of authority. Be careful, though, don't take it too far. You don't want to appear bossy, especially when you're just trying to help get things done in the most economical and productive way. Because you are sure of your good intentions, you can be deeply hurt when others find you forceful and impatient. Don't let your natural pride lead you to interpret questioning as criticism, especially by digging in your heels and refusing to budge from your position. Listen to others' points of view, even when you're

Prominent, high cheekbones

Angled-down cheekbones

Nice, large cheekbones

Angular and sharp cheekbones

convinced you are right. Sometimes that's all it takes to strengthen your relationships. And when you are wrong, remember, it's not a big deal. Give yourself a break.

I recently came across a picture of a clean-shaven Abraham Lincoln and was astounded by his exceedingly large, prominent cheekbones. I'm used to recalling him with a beard, which softened his appearance and my awareness of his features. I am thankful that President Lincoln used his gifts, and challenges, of extreme pride and confidence to do what he knew best, no matter what the opposition—nor any well-intended advice that may have come his way to lighten up.

To be a great leader it helps to be quick, efficient, astute, and decisive. Those with **angular and sharp cheekbones** are the perfect candidates. I love to work with these people. They meet their deadlines and don't lose their cool in emergencies. They're also great to be around when I get overwhelmed by too many choices. While I can spend more time than I care to admit discerning the many attributes of which restaurant to go to, my sharp-, angular-cheekboned friends have made the decision and the reservations, and have the car running and waiting.

If you have sharp, angular cheekbones, your challenge is your sharp words and criticisms. You might think you are only clearly expressing your opinion, but if you are frequently ruffling feathers, that might be why. Try a softer approach in tone and choice of words and see if you get what you want with more cooperation.

It has become popular lately in some circles to have cheekbone implants. If you succumb to this temptation, your new sharp and angled surgical implants could present a unique problem. Others will suddenly be looking to you for the answers, to lead them with what they subconsciously perceive as your innate gift. But the truth is that you now have a false authority that will confuse others and frustrate both them and you. This is another good example of "be careful what you wish for."

My student who is a former model suggested that people should have cheek implants that are fleshy so that it would soften the way in which others received their newfound authority. I had to agree, though I would rather we all lived with our given gifts and challenges and learned the lessons they give to us.

As you can imagine, people who have small or **flat cheekbones** not only lack the gift of authority, but it can be a mighty challenge for them to obtain a leadership role even when they are qualified, especially if they do not have other natural strong gifts such as determination, will, or passion. I know a wonderful, caring woman who loves children and has exceptional gifts of understanding and compassion. It would appear that her decision to open a preschool was perfect for her—except that her cheekbones are so flat they are nearly nonexistent. No matter what she said at the school, she was questioned—by the three-year-olds, the five-year-olds, most of the parents, and her own staff. Even though she owned the school and was highly intelligent and educated, it seemed that no one listened to her without challenging her authority. One year after opening her dream school, she sadly closed the doors. I'm happy to say that her

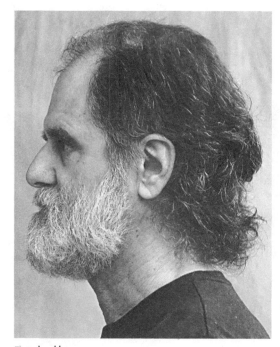

Flat cheekbones

story has a happy ending: She went back to school, earned a second Ph.D. in child development, and writes innovative curricula for schools across the country. Her authority is not questioned when she removes herself physically. She now sits back and lets her creative and commanding voice shine through in her books.

An artist I know with flat cheekbones is successful in his field as well as head of his department at a local college. He leads not by authority, but by the example of his passion, inspiration, and vibrant personality. I have actually heard him say that he disdains authority; he doesn't like to be told what to do, and he refuses to tell anyone else what to do. I think that's why his students are so creative and adventurous and have such great respect for him.

The set of prominent or high cheekbones gives us a clue as to how people use their authority. The **closer the cheekbones are set to the nose,** the more likely those people will give you warning before they give you an ultimatum. But, if those prominent cheekbones are **set back** closer to their ears, they expect you to react quickly and compliantly with their authority. When they tell you to do something, they expect it done now, with no excuses. If you have prominent, set-back cheekbones, you of course have the gift of pride (because of their prominence). Be aware to use this gift positively. Don't fall into the trap of thinking that a conflicting opinion is a challenge. Stop and listen fully and use your instinctive generous nature to step back from your position if necessary.

A woman who goes to our local café is the sweetest, most agreeable person I know. Her prominent cheekbones are set back, but I have a hard time imagining her

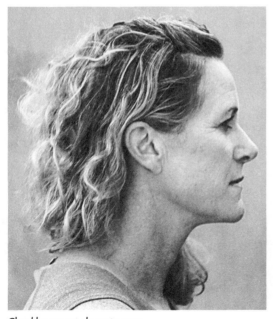

Cheekbones set closer to nose

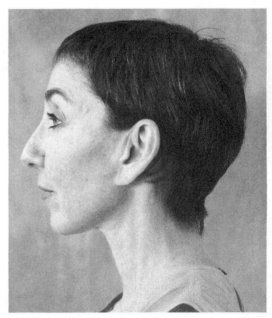

Cheekbones set back closer to ears

being prideful or snapping at anyone for not following her directions immediately or without question. When I asked her about this, she winced. "I am unbelievably impatient and snappish," she said, "but it's with my own self. I have zero tolerance for me. When I set a goal, I have to finish it ahead of time, and it has to be even more perfect than my original perfect plan! I have an inner dialogue like this: 'Do it now, do it better, do it faster; what are you waiting for!?'"

"Stop it," I said playfully, shaking a finger at her. "Be as sweet and patient to yourself as you are to everyone else."

She smiled sweetly. "If only it were that easy. But I'll remember what you've told me about our gifts and challenges and see if I can work through this one."

Remember the significance of the right and left sides of the face and features. If someone has a more prominent right cheekbone, consider their mother's influence regarding their use of authority, as well as how they choose to convey their outward expression of authority and how that might differ from how they actually feel inside. Another consideration is that they may like to act bossy to cover up how timid they might actually feel. My friend has a higher right cheekbone and I know from experience that deep inside she isn't confident about her authority, but she is good at *acting* authoritative when she needs to, especially in her career and with her young children.

A bigger left cheekbone indicates someone who is authoritative, but doesn't want to announce it or act on it. Perhaps demonstrating their authority was severely discouraged when they were a child and they are still hesitant about acting on that power, or perhaps they would rather wait and observe the situation before they take action.

> *Hollywood actress Joan Crawford may have started*
> *a trend among actresses and models when in the*
> *1940s she had her back teeth removed to make*
> *her cheekbones more prominent.*

NOSE

power/ego/drive/leadership grief Metal lungs white early to late 40s

The nose knows. It sits right there, in the middle of your face, playing a key role in telling the world who you are. Despite what the Earth personality believes, we do not live by bread alone. We need air. And our nose transports it down to our lungs, transporting it, filtering it, and warming it on its journey. If something gets trapped during this filtration, we sneeze it away—at more than one hundred miles per hour! That's some powerful proboscis we've got.

Smell is an invaluable primitive sense. It alerts us if our house is on fire, or to the sexy, sensual scent of the person next to us in the café. And it has a lot to do with other appetites. Without smell, we cannot taste as acutely. If we are nosy, we will find out the answer to many mysteries.

In Mien Shiang our nose tells the world how much ego, power, drive, and leadership we have. As with all the features, size is the indicator, and in this case size tells us if someone wants to be "out there" or hang back and blend in with the crowd.

One of the top ten questions I am asked in my workshops is whether reshaping your nose affects your personality. I am convinced it does. And more than one actor or entertainer's career has taken a nosedive after he reduced the size of his nose. The nose is the subliminal symbol of power, ego, drive, and leadership in most all cultures. When you make your nose smaller, you are perceived as less strong. I believe Michael Jackson's huge popularity and power began to recede at the same time, and as fast, as his nose did.

ALWAYS CONSIDER THE **METAL ELEMENT** ASSOCIATIONS FOR THE **NOSE**

characteristics	power, ego, drive, leadership
emotion	grief
element	Metal
organ	lungs
color	white
ages	early to late forties

Size

large nose	power, leader, drive, ego, independent
small nose	imaginative, spontaneous, fun, naïve, outbursts
disproportionately large nose	strong survival skills, self-centered, very independent

The **larger** the nose, the more power, ego, drive, leadership, and desire to work independently. The United States is full of large-nosed people: migrants, pioneers,

and adventurers who have overcome great obstacles to carve out a new life in a strange and often unreceptive country.

People with **small noses** frequently ask me if that means they do not have enough power, ego, and drive to be effective leaders. The answer of course is that anyone can be a leader, even a great leader, no matter the size of his or her nose (or other features). Large-nosed people have the gift of leadership traits, so they don't have to struggle; they are natural leaders. The rest of us who don't have those gifts merely have to work harder, more diligently, or maybe longer to obtain those goals. We can also partner with large-nosed people who are looking to us for our natural gifts that complement their

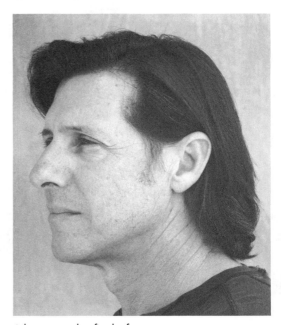

A large nose that fits the face

challenges. Of course, if you have a small nose but prominent cheeks and cheekbones, your gifts of confidence and authority will more easily propel you to leadership roles. Or perhaps your Water features, such as a prominent forehead signaling your creative imagination, and your strong, determined jaws, are all the natural gifts you need to be in the lead.

Many with small noses don't care to be leaders. They are best in group activities where they use their creative imaginations and spontaneity. Their challenge is that

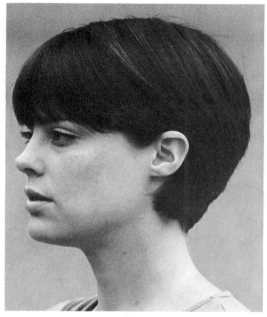
A small nose that fits the face

they can be naïve visionaries, impatient for results. This leads to frustration, which can lead to temper outbursts. Even so, they do think of others and are always willing to help out for the greater good, usually making the task fun. They love to play and have to love what they do in order to work hard.

I first met Paolo several years ago at a friend's party. He was in his midthirties, quite handsome, exceedingly charming, and spoke several languages. I was hardly surprised to see him surrounded by admirers all evening. But I was surprised to learn that he was president of a hot new start-up company that was making news all over Los Angeles. He had been entertaining us with the stories behind the headlines all evening, and I had been studying his face. I had a hunch about something so I sought out our hostess.

Christine had known Paolo for years, so I asked her if by any chance this eminently successful company of his was co-owned by a family member? "Oh, yes," she said, pointing to a man of about forty who had recently arrived. "His brother Stefan is the CEO—and the brains behind it all. He lets Paolo be president or vice president of all his companies."

Paolo had such a small nose that I had suspected he was more a figurehead than an innovative business leader. His great gift was his charisma, and I'm sure he brought much initial attention and interest to the company with this charm. I also knew that no matter how much fun it was to start a business, to keep it thriving you had to work very hard. Once the fun is gone, often so is the small-nosed person. Within months I heard that Paolo had suddenly left the company to travel in South America. Luckily, he has several successful family members scattered across a few continents and has had much fun over the years enjoying his impressive titles at many of these family businesses.

Here is a case in Mien Shiang where more *is* too much: **Disproportionately large-nosed** persons, those whose large nose is much too big for their face, are self-centered, thinking of themselves first, second, and always. Their strong survival instincts make them great adventurers. They are not good team players and not very good leaders, either, but they wouldn't agree. They are better off working independently.

Length

long nose	business-oriented, good sense, success, ambitious, proud
short nose	loyal, compassion, wary, difficulty committing

The nose of Thomas Wedders, the English circus performer, was seven and a half inches long.

The **longer** your nose, the prouder you are, and for good reason. You have a good nose for business, common sense, a healthy sense of ambition, great instincts, and people respond positively to your leadership. Your biggest problems are often derived from your greatest strengths. Your tendency to resent those who do not show appreciation for all of your tireless efforts can cause dissension in the workplace. Be careful not to look down your lovely long nose at those who do not have the same natural sense of fairness and justice that you have. And remember, family life does not need to run with the same efficiency as your work life. In fact, it shouldn't. Trust that having fun is good for you and your family.

Short-nosed people are loyal and compassionate, but generally short on drive and ambition. They just don't have the emotional stamina to thrive in competitive conditions and are often wary and overwhelmed by those who have strong egos and drive. They like the results that the aggressive types get, and this can lead to frustration, even resentment, and a

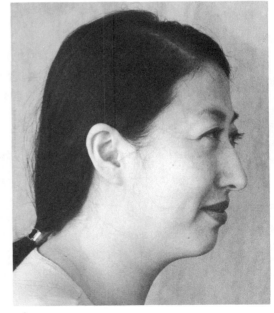

A long nose

A short nose (but the strong chin gives the subject a strong will)

rough time committing to anything. A colleague of mine, Janos, has a short nose, but a strong ego, plenty of drive, and natural leadership. He is like so many other people who are "shorted" by one gift, but make up for it with others. Janos's prominent eyebrows denote his intense passion, his high-angled cheekbones reveal his natural authority, and he has the most determined jaws on the planet. If his nose were any longer, I am convinced his ego and drive would be much too overwhelming. He's just right the way he is.

Set and Positioning

high-set nose	ambitious, proud, energetic, pacesetter, self-reliant, doesn't like rules
low-set nose	loyal, traditional, good partner, family-oriented

My friend Brian is a social activist and agitator with the **highest-set nose** of anyone I've ever met. The gift of the high-set nose is primarily ambition, and no one can match his when it comes to his crusade to eliminate hunger and empower the poor and oppressed in his own country. This nose certainly "comes off his face," which the ancient Taoists considered necessary to be a warrior and leader; it reflects his self-reliance, abundant energy, and righteous pride to confront hostility and demand change without fear of intimidation. This is not a nose that goes by the rules. In fact, I would call it a revolutionary nose.

The Taoist monks claimed that people who have **low-set or flat, close noses** are not so interested in being leaders. But they do like working for powerful leaders who have clearly defined values and expectations that they can plug right into. Their loyalty is a valuable asset, but it can lead them astray if the leaders they admire lose their own moral ground.

Derek, a former student of mine, has a low-set nose. Last year, while in his third year of studying Traditional Chinese Medicine, he realized that the homeless and poor of Los Angeles' downtown skid row would benefit immensely from acupuncture treatments. Unfortunately, he could find no acupuncture clinics on skid row where he could volunteer his skills. So, this man with a low-set nose quickly gathered six of his fellow Traditional Chinese Medicine students and a licensed practitioner from Yo San University and headed down to skid row, needles, herbs, and nutritious food in hand. That was the beginning of the continuing mobile clinic that draws together more clients, practitioners, and students each time. If that isn't leadership, what is? The difference that I detect between the leader with the high-set nose and one with the low-set nose is the high energy versus the low-key energy; the tearing away at boundaries versus the pushing for new paths; the self-reliant warrior versus the team player. Which is better? Neither, of course. They both create momentous transformation in their own vital way.

A high-set nose

A low-set nose

Shape

narrow nose	narrow outlook and range of interests, conservative with money
thin nose	sensitive, moody, intuitive, self-centered, refined, easily influenced
sharp and pointed nose	a nose for news
broad nose	enthusiastic, sensual, optimistic, dependable, capable
straight nose	loyal, successful, disciplined, impatient, appearance important, fair

Be careful not to confuse the narrow outlook and narrow range of interests of the **narrow nose** person with narrow-mindedness. These people tend to be mega-experts, honing in on the most detailed, esoteric specifics of their chosen interests.

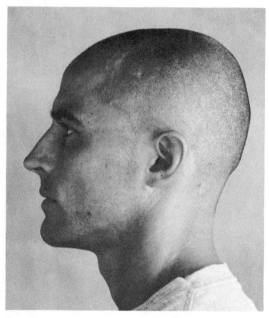

A narrow nose

They do not like to spend money frivolously or frequently. Nominate them for your club or class treasurer, but don't expect them to join you for an impromptu weekend trip to Paris for shopping.

A **thin nose** *is* different from a narrow nose, but it is a fine distinction. Once you get used to looking at thousands of noses, you will begin to see the subtle differences. In Mien Shiang a thin nose means that the bone and cartilage seem delicate or fragile, and the skin stretches so tightly over the nose that it appears it might tear. A student once noted that many nose jobs have this look, and I have to agree with her. The description for those with thin noses sounds like the prototype for the country-club set: refined, elegant, delicate, with impeccable taste. One of their challenges is that they are easily influenced regarding issues of taste, propriety, and trends. This desire to be proper, appropriate, and perfect can make them appear self-centered. When they find themselves too dependent on others' opinions, they need to rely on their astute intuition. Their occasional moodiness seems to be more snappish than heavy or depressed, not making them good candidates to be nurtured out of their moods. They would rather be left alone to sort things out.

Do you have a thin nose that is particularly **sharp and pointed**? Then you have a great nose for news. With your natural inquisitiveness and probing nature, you would make a great investigative reporter. Or at least a popular person in your social and work groups because you know all the stories and fine details about everyone and everything.

A thin, sharp, and pointed nose

A few years ago an energetic vegetarian nutritionist with a thin, sharp, and pointed nose attended my workshop at a beautiful California coastal resort. She was hoping this Mien Shiang workshop would help her learn enough about the Five Elements for her to create fitting menus for her clients based on their elemental types. I loved her enthusiasm and ingenuity, but the other workshop attendees were becoming perturbed with her frequent interruptions to apply my teachings to her specific needs. She amiably agreed to hold some of her questions for our breaks, and to e-mail me later in the week. I thanked her, then added, "By the way, you have what we call a wonderful nose for news."

"I should have," she answered, rolling her eyes. "I was an award-winning journalist for fifteen years."

"I have a feeling you're going to be an award-winning nutritionist, too," I told her. My guess is that by now there is nothing she does not know about any fruit or vegetable, from avocados to zucchinis, and that she can apply all of the details of the Five Elements to her culinary creations.

If you have a **broad nose,** you might be the one to take off on that impromptu intercontinental shopping spree. You love to be on the go and will enthusiastically take advantage of as many opportunities for pleasure as you can. Though you can get lost

A broad nose

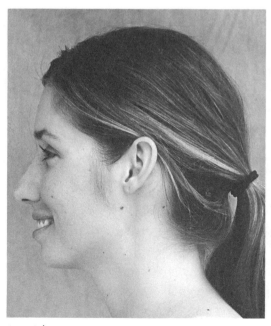

A straight nose

in sensual pursuits, you know your limits. Your many friends depend on you, and you don't let them down.

Besides the thin-nosed people, you will see a lot of **straight-nosed** people in the country-club sets, especially among the Metal personalities. Something about the straight nose looks elegant and regal. Perhaps that is why these people are often thought of as being snobbish, even when they are the most egalitarian people on the planet, though it is true that appearance and appearances are quite important to them. They are always impeccably dressed, and their homes and offices are attractive and neat as a pin. They value their relationships and are disciplined, fair-minded employers and employees. Though they are impatient by nature, they are not snappish or rude.

Success seems to come easily to the straight-nosed person. It doesn't hurt that their friends, coworkers, and family frequently offer help and advice.

I knew an exceptionally straight-nosed woman who was intent on climbing the social ladder. Though Margot didn't yet have the income or affiliations she needed to reach the top, she looked fabulous. She worked hard on looking the part, and that alone helped her attain a few rungs on her climb. One day she was trying to explain to me why our mutual friend Lydia couldn't be invited to her holiday dinner party. "You mean she's not coming because she doesn't *look* right?" I asked, thinking I was teasing Margot.

"Well, yes," she nodded, relieved that I finally understood. "I'm hoping to get appointed to the board of the museum, and two of the members will be at the party. You can imagine what impression I would make if I had a shopgirl at the table, dressed like a ragamuffin."

"She's been your friend for thirty years," I protested. "She'll be crushed."

"Of course she won't. She understands how these things work. Besides, I'm having another party the next week and she'll be my guest of honor."

Before I could protest further, I remembered that Lydia also had a precision-straight nose; she most likely did understand how these things work. And both she and Margot had considered each other loyal and trustworthy friends for many years. I decided to mind my own business.

An interesting addendum: Since my friend's appointment to the board of the museum, I haven't been invited to any of her dinner parties. Oh, dear.

> *Three thousand years ago the ancient Taoists believed*
> *that large-nosed women would make their husbands*
> *successful, and the small-nosed women would nurture*
> *their husbands to success. In these modern times,*
> *those women use these same skills to make or*
> *nurture their own successes.*

Tip of the Nose

rounded tip	material pleasures
fleshy tip	quality, gourmand
split tip	split feelings of materialism

A **rounded nose** belongs to the material girls or boys. They are not greedy, but they appreciate things of quality. They would rather go without than put up with an inferior substitute.

If you love good-quality food and drink, you most likely have a gourmand's nose, one with a **fleshy tip.** If you don't have one yourself, these are the people to dine with. Let them choose the restaurant and the menu. Sit back and enjoy.

People with either fleshy or rounded tips of their noses that are **split** (bigger on

A true gourmand's nose, round and fleshy

A nose with a split tip

one side than the other) have split feelings about their love of things and food. It might be their guilt that keeps them from completely enjoying themselves. A student once said he was glad that the end of his fleshy nose had a little split in the middle. Otherwise, he was sure he would be very overweight.

Markings on the Nose

REMINDER ABOUT FACIAL MARKINGS

Markings such as scars, lines, and some discolorations are acquired, while others, such as moles and birthmarks, can be inherited.

Markings on the left or right sides of the face reveal father's or mother's influence as well as your own inner or outer personality and behavior.

Markings on the tip of the nose reflect the emotions of the heart. If the markings are red, it means the feelings are inflamed or highly emotional. Greenish or brown markings usually indicate that not only is the heart hurt, but anger is attached to that heartache.

A few years ago we were discussing these markings in class at Yo San University, and the next week Jason, one of my students, came in a little bit late, after everyone else was seated. Before I knew it, his classmate Vivien called out, "Oh, goodness, Jason, you have a heartbreak!"

Jason's cheeks turned as red as the bright dot on the tip of his nose. He ignored the comment and slumped into his seat. I gave the rest of the class a nod to let them know that we would not pursue Vivien's comment, and to please stop trying to catch a look at the tip of poor Jason's nose! (Not that the round, vivid red dot on the left side of the tip of his nose was hard to miss—it was a classic.)

During the class break all the students rushed out of the classroom, except Jason. Sure enough, he told me, his heart had been broken a few days ago and he was suffering. All I could do was offer my sympathy and remind him of his good qualities and strengths, which were many. I also pointed out that since the red dot was on his left side, he might want to be careful of keeping his feelings too closely guarded inside himself. "I know you are intensely private, but remember to let those close to you know you need their help right now; don't try and do this alone," I urged him.

Jason gave me a long, sardonic look, then said, "Like I could keep any secrets from this class. Face reading—harrumph!"

To his immense credit, when we resumed class, Jason offered to sit in the "hot seat" so that his fellow students could observe the marking on the tip of his nose, and for the next few weeks he let them monitor it, confirming their educated guesses that as the red dot grew paler and smaller, so did his heartbreak. It took a while, though. I was happy that by being a dedicated acupuncture student Jason was able to get the support he needed.

Inevitably, whenever I teach about the tip of the nose and the heart's emotions, someone will ask me about Michael Jackson. It has been reported, and pictures do seem to confirm, that he has literally lost the tip of his nose. They will ask, "Does that affect his heart emotions?" Since I do not know Mr. Jackson, nor do I know much about his personal life, I am of course reluctant to speak as an expert on his emotions of the heart. But I do admit that I would be shocked if the constant reshaping and eventual loss of his nose tip has not had a harrowing effect on his heart. I fear that he could indeed be in perpetual heartache.

FA LING LINES

Our Fa Ling lines, also called Purpose Lines, tell us if we are aware of our creative and spiritual purpose in life, if we have strong ideals, and to what extent we are following our true goals. Because they reflect our ability to eliminate the superfluous issues that bog us down and to nurture our essential talents, we should have Fa Ling lines by our early to mid-forties.

I have seen several sculptures of Socrates, and he has the most beautiful Fa Ling lines. It certainly appears, just from his face alone, that he knew his creative and spiritual purpose in life.

We don't want the Fa Ling lines to be too deep or too long. They generally begin next to the top of the nostrils and flare gently downward, forming soft commas that end before reaching the corners of the mouth. The length, depth, and specific shape vary with each person, and with each side of the face, but they should fall within these parameters. They can appear on both sides, or on just one side.

If you have a Fa Ling line only on your left side, then you have a true inner awareness and belief in your life's purpose, but you are not yet living according to your full creative and spiritual potential. Ask yourself what is keeping you from fulfilling what you know to be your true life pur-

Fa Ling lines are a good length and depth

The Fa Ling line on the left side is longer and deeper

pose, and how you can get on what the ancient Taoists called your Full Life Path.

A Fa Ling line only on the right side indicates that you are actually living the creative and spiritual life you are meant to live, but something, or someone, is keeping you from valuing your life's path. Oftentimes our family, culture, or community does not approve of who we are, and it is not easy to shake off their judgments. It may take enormous courage to live your life according to your own beliefs, but the rewards are immeasurable. You have only one life to live on this journey; make it yours.

Though it is fashionable in our culture to erase the lines on our face, it is tragic to remove the evidence that we are on our creative and spiritual path. Look around and see how many others are still seeking theirs and be thankful for your beautiful Fa Ling lines.

When Fa Ling lines are deep, they are called **Over-Purpose lines.** They are caused by trying too hard to find your creative and spiritual path. The real issue is control. Sometimes you have to let go; open your heart and soul and let your creativity and spirit find you or at least meet you halfway.

Over-Purpose lines become **Disappointment lines** when they extend far below the corners of the mouth. They come when disappointment from past failures stops you from seeking your life's purpose.

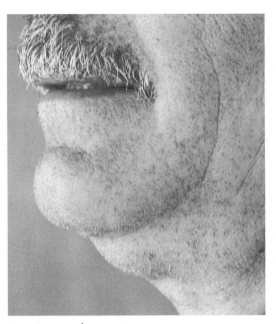

Disappointment lines

Fa Ling lines that fall low—if due to stress or overwork, they will shorten when stress is alleviated

Once in a while, when we are going through a particularly stressful time, our Fa Ling lines will deepen or suddenly extend too low. But once the stress is alleviated, the lines fade back to their normal depth and length.

Sometimes these lines fall way below each side of the mouth and meet on the chin, forming a circle. We call this a **Starvation line** because that person is starving for love and approval. I have seen this line fade away as soon as people begin to approve of themselves enough to love and be loved by another. It's amazing how quickly love heals.

PHILTRUM

creativity worry Earth stomach brown/yellow early 50s

The philtrum is the vertical groove in the middle of the upper lip between the top lip and the nose. Its name comes from the Greek *philtron*, which means "love potion," and was so named because the ancient Greeks believed this was one of the most erogenous zones of the body.

The philtrum mustache was made quite popular by silent-screen star Charlie Chaplin, but it fell out of favor when Hitler began to sport one. In recent years Robert Mugabe, president of Zimbabwe, wears an extremely narrow one, covering only the philtrum and nothing to either side.

In Mien Shiang we look at the philtrum to determine creativity, emotional aspects of fertility and desire for children, stress, and sensitivity.

short philtrum	do not like to be teased
long philtrum	like to be teased
long and deep philtrum	intense desire for children/creativity
horizontal lines across philtrum	cutting off of creativity or fertility/postmenopausal

If you have a **short philtrum,** you certainly do not like to be teased. You have probably been called touchy, especially if you grew up with impish siblings.

Those with a **long philtrum** not only do not mind being teased, they love it.

They love practical jokes, even if they are the target; they're the ideal good sports about everything.

A **long, deep philtrum** indicates an intense desire, or even need, for children as well as creativity. If you have a long and deep philtrum yet do not have children, you will find yourself almost parentally nurturing your creative projects and works.

Horizontal lines cutting across the philtrum represent the cutting off of creativity, and in some cases the cutting off of fertility or desire for children, especially noticeable in postmenopausal women.

A beautifully spirited woman in her late thirties who attended one of my workshops last year had a distinct **vertical line** in the middle of her philtrum. Since I knew that she did not have children, I asked if she might be worried about her creativity or a creative project in particular. She was quite sure neither was the case.

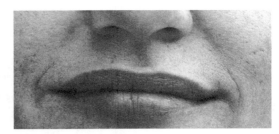

A short, deep philtrum

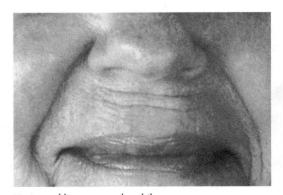

Horizontal lines across the philtrum

Later in the weekend when the group was reading her face, we learned that she had had an intensely traumatic childhood, mostly due to the erratic and violent behavior of her schizophrenic mother. It became clear to me then that the worry that her vertical philtrum line represented was of having a child of her own.

When I asked her if she had decided not to have children, she exclaimed, "Oh,

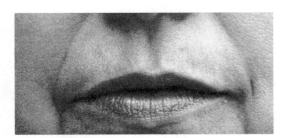

A long philtrum

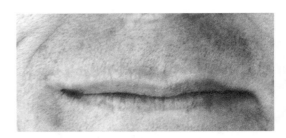

A smooth upper lip with no noticeable philtrum

definitely yes! I've always worried that I would inherit my mother's illness, and I would never forgive myself for inflicting the same terror that I grew up with onto my own child."

Several months later she attended another of my classes and showed me that her philtrum line had lightened, as had her worries. She was so relieved to have shared her story and fears that she was looking forward to letting go of all her past fears and trauma and moving forward in her life. She is a lovely woman and I have no doubt she will bring many healing and creative aspects into her continuing healthy life.

MOUTH

personality worry Earth stomach yellow mid 50s, 60, and mid 60s

Our mouth is our most mobile and obviously functional facial feature. Our lips form the words of speech, which is perhaps our best communication skill. Twist and turn your mouth and you have a smile, pout, sneer, frown, or snarl.

Lips make eating and drinking easy, especially if we are using a straw. We even have a special etiquette for the mouth, which every child (we hope) has heard on occasion: Don't chew with your mouth open!

And let's not forget kissing. Ever.

In the Taoist study of the face the mouth tells us about our personality, intellect, feelings and love, sexuality and sensuality.

ALWAYS CONSIDER THE **EARTH ELEMENT** ASSOCIATIONS FOR THE **MOUTH**

characteristic	personality
emotion	worry
element	Earth
organ	stomach
color	yellow
ages	midfifties, sixty, and midsixties

The **ideal mouth** is slightly moist, symmetrical, clearly defined, with a straight line between the lips, and uplifted corners.

Sizes and Shapes of Lips and Mouth

large mouth	generous, large appetites, big personality
large, full mouth	earthy, generous, likes attention, likes teasing, likes adoration
small mouth	self-centered, strong-willed
wide mouth	sensual, need to be happy, lively, jealous
narrow mouth	head rules the heart, fragile health
thin lips	too much control, sensual over sexual, more intellectual, dislikes teasing
very thin top lip	calculating, creative
fuller top lip	epicurean, poetic, romantic, desires emotional drama
fuller lower lip	self-reliant, strong ego, successful, sensual, desires physical pleasure
protruding top lip	insecure, difficult childhood
protruding bottom lip	quiet, for the underdog, levelheaded, devoted to family
extremely protruding bottom lip	brash, successful, sexually adventurous
points in lips	refined, sensitive, delicate, sensitive to outside stimuli
crooked mouth	stretch the truth
open mouth	easily influenced, need mentors
half-open mouth	warm, generous
tightly closed mouth	compassionate, fearful of speaking own truth, blames self

People with a **large mouth** often have large personalities. Their appetites for all the earthly pleasures combined with their natural generosity pretty much guarantee them a large circle of friends.

A **large, full mouth** has been a symbol of cinema's sex goddesses from Brigitte Bardot's famous pout to Angelina Jolie's alluring lips. What most of these

A full mouth

screen idols also have in common is their need for attention. These are people who love to be teased and be the object of any fun-loving attention; they consider it flirting of sorts. I don't know if they fit the other Taoist traits for large and full mouths of being faithful only if adored, completely satisfied by, and shamelessly doted on by their mate. I'm sure one of the gossip magazines could fill us in on that. Those with fuller lips are also earthier than most; they just love their earthly pleasures, especially food and sex.

High levels of estrogen in females are related to
health and fertility, and biologists predict that
males will seek out females with signs of high
estrogen levels, such as full lips.

Small mouths belong to those who have difficulty relating to another's point of view or circumstances. The smaller the mouth, the more hypersensitive they are

A small mouth

about not getting what they perceive as their due. Unfortunately, they tend to have an overinflated sense of their worth so they are constantly imagining themselves as victims who need to fight for their rights. They are not embarrassed to thrust themselves into the center of any attention to get their own self-interests met. Consider yourself lucky if you are on the same team with them as your interests will become theirs, and they are tenacious in their pursuits.

I have a friend who has a small mouth, but his Fire personality gives him sparkle, warmth, and fun, as well as a genuine concern for others to offset the self-centered challenges of his small mouth. He fights more for the good of the whole rather than for only himself. And though he is tenacious, he is never rude and is always honest.

On the other hand, I know a woman whose very small mouth is set tightly on her face. Her innate challenge is not easy, and only great desire and effort on her part will alter her confrontational and provoking behavior so that she may eventually have a healthy life. Unfortunately, she is so dominated by the Wood element, with thick, heavy eyebrows and brow bones, and essentially no other elemental influences, that it is a monumental struggle for her to balance her feelings and actions. Since being angry and confrontational makes her feel energized, it is as though she has become addicted to these behaviors. While her path is not an easy one, her rewards could be great if she meets her challenges head-on rather than looking for conflict and control.

People with **wide mouths** laugh a lot, showing off their naturally great smiles. They are lively, sensual people who need

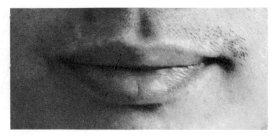
A wide mouth

to be showered with love. If you have a warm and invitingly wide mouth, enjoy the rewards that your lively, happy personality brings to you and others, but be aware of your tendency toward jealousy, which can make for many short-lived romances.

(For all of my exact Metal friends who like to know the precise measurements of all things, a wide mouth is more than 55 mm for men and 47 mm for women. A narrow mouth is less than 50 mm wide for men and 40 mm wide for women.)

The head rules the heart of people with a **narrow mouth.** Overall, they are more practical than passionate, and their fragile health may contribute to their settled lifestyle. If your mouth is narrow, literally practice smiling more. It will widen your mouth and make you and everyone around you feel better.

A narrow mouth

Years ago guerrilla artist Robbie Conal papered all of Los Angeles with his poster drawings of famous politicians and titled the series *Men with No Lips*. That was when I first became aware just how many politicians do have very **thin lips;** their mouths look like thin slashes underscoring their noses. Some would say that the traits of thin lips—having stringent control over emotions, needs, and thoughts—are positive for a politician. Others might think quite the opposite.

They are more sensual than sexual in their romantic pursuits and tend to intellectualize everything, even their love lives. If you want to have fun with thin-lipped people, don't even think of teasing them; they'll be certain you're making fun of them—not with them.

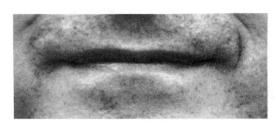
Thin lips

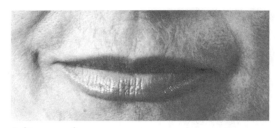

A thinner top lip

A fuller top lip

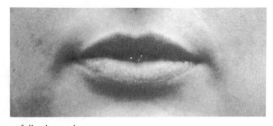

A fuller lower lip

If you see people with a **very thin top lip** (compared to their lower lip), you can be sure they are creative, sensible, and make clear and calculated decisions.

People with a **fuller top lip** than their bottom one are earthy. Dedicated epicureans, they will go to any length for great food. They are romantic poets who have difficulty finding the perfect love. But they love the intense drama of the hunt (they can be the proverbial drama queens or kings) and are known as great lovers; it's probably all the experience.

Sixty percent of men have a **fuller lower lip** (than their top lip), so I cannot help but wonder about an ancient interpretation one of my teachers had found in a dusty book in Taiwan years ago: unreliable, high opinion of self (which it said is often undeserved!), gift of gab, unlucky in love, and sensual. Thank goodness the more commonly known traits are self-reliant, strong ego, successful, and sensual. Unlike those with fuller upper lips, who are enticed by the exciting emotional drama of sex and love, they are more interested in the straightforward physical pleasures of the pursuit and expression of love.

Those with a **protruding top lip** have a wistful insecurity, making it hard to get to know them. As children they had to put everyone else in the family first, so they've never learned to stand up for themselves. They will go to any lengths to avoid aggression and confrontation. They appear to be unsensual, but with the right partner they can slowly learn to enjoy intimacy. They don't want to talk about it, though.

Recently, I was leaving my favorite downtown-Tucson coffee spot when a small but threatening group of people demanded money from me. This type of aggression is rare in this charming desert city and I was taken aback, especially when one woman grabbed and squeezed my arm when I tried to walk on by. I followed my immediate instinct to turn back into the little café and summon the owner. If anyone could defuse this situation levelheadedly and without fuss it was he. His **slightly protruding lower lip** indicates a willingness to stand up for others even at his own risk. Though he's quiet about his own wants, he will never hesitate to speak up for and protect others, particularly the underdog. What I especially valued in him in this event is that he broke up the circle of aggression outside his café without demeaning the aggressors and escalating the situation. He was respectful to all. People love to work for people with the slightly protruding lower lip because their fairness

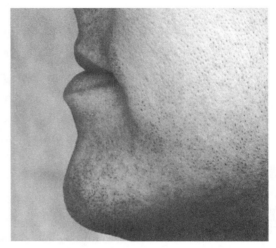

A slightly protruding lower lip

and respect leads to a pleasant and profitable workplace. They tend to have a small circle of friends, preferring to spend time with family, where they are valued as loyal and devoted mates, children, and siblings.

As helpful as people with a slightly protruding lower lip are, those with an **extremely protruding lower lip** have an almost reverse personality. They tend to be brash, and their many successes come from pushing their way to the front regardless of the consequences to others. They are not romantic, but quite sexually adventurous. It doesn't bother them if their mates have affairs also, as long as they themselves are free to do as they please.

I asked a medical student in one of my workshops who claimed to have frequented swingers' clubs while in college if she had noticed many extreme protruding bottom lips. She didn't remember, but she said that both of her surgical residents fit the physical and behavioral descriptions of this feature. A hush filled the room while a few of the students turned to look at the back of the room. Unknown to the medical student, one of those residents was sitting in the back row. I hoped fervently that the medical student hadn't had her heart set on pursuing surgery as a specialty.

Points in the lips belong to refined, sensitive, and delicate people who are

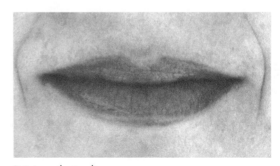

Points on the top lip

aware of everything around them. They are highly sensitive to any stimuli and often pick up others' unspoken feelings and attitudes.

Crooked mouth, crooked thoughts.
OLD CHINESE SAYING

The ancients said that those who constantly stretch the truth will eventually stretch their lips, giving them **crooked mouths.** These poor people can't keep their mouths closed, even for their own good. Though those who habitually stretch the truth are dishonest, crafty, and sly, every once in a while people who are basically honest will have a crooked mouth, and they will have a hard time convincing others of their truthfulness and sincerity. Note that a mouth that is higher or thinner, lower or thicker, on one side or the other is not a crooked mouth. A crooked mouth is so crooked that it appears distorted, and I've seen few of these.

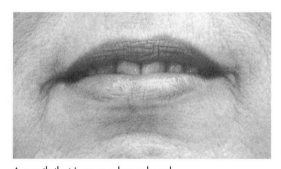

A mouth that is open when relaxed

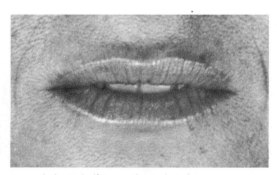

A mouth that is half-open when relaxed

If, when at rest, your **mouth is open,** be careful of being easily influenced by others. You have most likely always been on the naïve side and were slow to mature. Learn to trust your own instincts and develop your own skills so that you are less dependent on the role models and mentors whom you are constantly seeking.

A **mouth that is half- or even slightly open** while at rest is just right in that it belongs to an open and generous person. These are warm, friendly, and energetic people who have a great gift of understanding the needs and wants of others.

A **tightly closed mouth** tells us that the person's thoughts, feelings, and words are held tightly in reserve. This often belongs to the person who was not allowed as a child to speak her mind or her truth. When you have to hold back the expression of your true voice, you will most likely keep your lips tightly pressed so nothing leaks out and lands you in trouble. These people become rigid in their behavior and are overly cautious about exposing their true selves, and who can blame them?

A mouth that is tightly closed when relaxed

If this is you, don't let those past repressive experiences saddle you with a victim mentality. When you haven't learned to be comfortable with yourself as a child, it's hard to learn to take responsibility for yourself when you are grown. The past can make you a king or queen of pessimism, or it can propel you toward confidence. Use your gift of compassion not just for others, but for yourself. Believe in your own truth, act on it, and see how wonderful it is to relax and not be afraid of being the complete you. You'll be surprised to see how much more energy of mind, body, and spirit you will suddenly have.

Set and Positioning

upturned mouth	optimism
downturned mouth	pessimism
mouth turned up, or fuller, on right	appear more optimistic than they feel; more sexual than they appear
mouth turned up, or fuller, on left	appear pragmatic, but truly an optimist; more sensual than they appear
pursed mouth	martyr, judgmental, punitive

Upturned mouths are universally interpreted as belonging to optimists, **downturned mouths** to pessimists. In ancient China, women with upturned mouths were said to have been blessed with a Courtesan's Mouth because the emperor's favorite courtesans had naturally upturned mouths, and they were said to always make the emperor feel better simply by their pleasing presence. Potential paramours with downturned mouths were

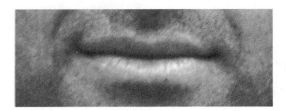

A naturally upturned mouth

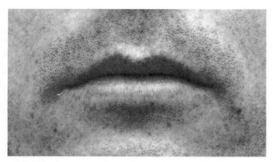

A slightly downturned mouth

turned away from the emperor's court because their negative attitude would not only displease the emperor, but would adversely affect the good nature of all the courtesans—all three thousand of them.

Wide-screen legend Bette Davis was known for her eyes, so much so that a song was even written about them. But I think her most notable feature was her downturned mouth. And it seems from the publicity surrounding her many personal conflicts, including those with her father and daughter, that she had many reasons to be downhearted and pessimistic.

My friend Tricia has the dilemma that many people with mouths that are **fuller or turned up on the right side only** have. No matter how many times or how emphatically she tells those close to her that she is sad, she doesn't get the compassion and nurturing she desires. With her little natural half-smile she just doesn't look that sad, so her needs are often ignored. I know this is a key reason for her ongoing low-grade depression, which few people in her life recognize as being as painful as it is to her. Her husband tries to stay attuned to her words and not be fooled by what he calls her curse of false perkiness, but admits that even he frequently forgets. She just *looks* so perky.

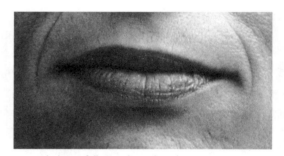

A mouth that is fuller on the right side

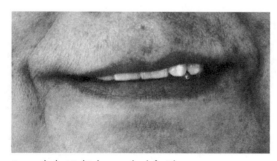

A mouth that is higher on the left side

Those with a **fuller or upturned mouth on the left side only** have the opposite problem, except it's not such a problem. They look like pragmatists, but inside they are actually optimists. As we commented early in this book, some cultures believe it is unwise or even unlucky to wear your feelings on your sleeve, so to speak. If you are by nature an upbeat, optimistic person, it will be hard for you to obey the rules of your culture and to keep your face thick and your heart black. So it would not be too surprising if the left side of your mouth was a wee bit upturned.

I have an acquaintance who is a professional gambler, and he asked me to study the faces of some of his opponents and give him some tips. I wasn't willing to go to Las Vegas or to any gambling clubs, but I did agree to watch a televised poker tournament with him one evening. I noticed right away an unusual preponderance of gamblers with the left side of their mouth upturned. For some it was part of their natural look, but for others it would occur intermittently. With one of the card players especially, we were pretty sure that his left mouth corner went up every time he had a good hand and was trying a big bluff.

Sucking on sour lemons is one way to get **pursed lips.** Another is to be perpetually sour on life with a martyred, judgmental, and punitive attitude. Not a favorite personality, but it seems most families have at least one of these sourpusses to take the enjoyment out of a happy event or two.

Markings on the Mouth

REMINDER ABOUT FACIAL MARKINGS

Markings such as scars, lines, and some discolorations are acquired, while others, such as moles and birthmarks, can be inherited.

Markings on the left or right sides of the face reveal father's or mother's influence as well as your own inner or outer personality and behavior.

lines around the mouth	resentment, overnurturing
lines cutting into top lip	holding on to past hurts
moles	luck or lack of it

Those **tiny lines around the mouth** are often called smoker's lines. True, some smokers do have these lines, but most don't. What those who have the lines do have in common is resentment. They belong to overnurturers who have given and given, but have never felt adequately thanked or appreciated. The reason is that those to

Lines cutting into the top lip

whom they gave so much to did not feel taken care of; they felt smothered. These overnurturers' generosity has a lot of "you owe me for all I've done for you" in it. Their adolescent and adult children are quite often looking to get away from the overbearing parent, rather than finding elaborate means to profess great thanks. Even when these children do offer their sincere thanks for all of the sacrifices made by their overnurturing parent, they find that their appreciation just isn't enough. Overnurturers are a bottomless pit when it comes to rewards and neediness.

We all know someone with **harsh lines cutting into their top lip.** Each of those lines represents a past hurt that has not been forgotten. If you see those lines forming on your lip, the sooner you deal with your past hurts and let them go, the sooner your life will fill with happiness and hope for the future. That sure beats ending up cold and bitter in your old age. Don't make your loved ones work hard to garner your acceptance and forgiveness. Give it to them generously and freely. No one will benefit more than you.

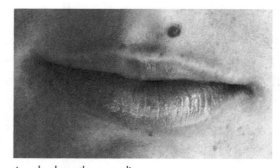

A mole above the upper lip

Moles near the edge of the mouth, especially the corners, are generally considered auspicious, giving a little boost to your personality, and if you are a woman, to your sexuality. If a mole cuts into the body of the lip, that could be letting you know of a challenge regarding your personality or sexuality. If the mole is on the right side

A mole on the upper lip

of your mouth, the challenge might be that you are often misunderstood because you have difficulty projecting your true personality and feelings to the outer world. If it is on the left side of the mouth, you might want to see if you are having a conflict in accepting the true nature of your personality or sexuality, or both.

straight line between lips	powerful, curious, need sexual challenge
wavy line between lips	self-confident/needs monetary security
crooked mouth	dishonest/stretch the truth

The line that forms between our two lips tells something about us, too. If you have **straight lips,** meaning that a straight line forms between your lips when they are closed, you have a curious and powerful personality and you will do anything to win or be right. Your head rules your heart, and you need a challenge romantically and sexually or you will soon lose interest.

A **wavy line** between the lips indicates self-confident and broad-minded people. They like attention and function best in all manners when they have financial security.

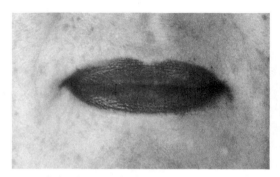

A straight line between the lips

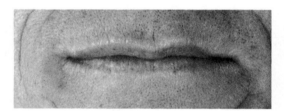

A wavy line between the lips

CHIN

*character/will worry Earth stomach yellow
early and late 60s, and early to mid 70s*

If you are down in the dumps, all you need to do is *chin up* and all will be well. *Taking it on the chin* means you won't back down. Neither of these are old Chinese expressions, but they do fit with the ancient Taoists' analysis of what our chins tell us about ourselves.

The traits of the chin are character and will. Most people interpret *will* to mean "stubborn," but the Taoist translation has more to do with your willingness to lead your life on your own terms rather than your tenaciousness. We're not all blessed with strong chins and strong will, but will can be developed. As with most things, the first step can be the hardest; that's the paradox, of course, to having this particular challenge. You have to want to make your own path in life and thereby accept the trials, tribulations, disappointments, and responsibilities that are bound to occur along the way. The Taoist monks told us that character is necessary for longevity, so as you develop your will, you'll also develop your character, and you will be rewarded with a long life—all on your own terms.

ALWAYS CONSIDER THE **EARTH ELEMENT** ASSOCIATIONS FOR THE **CHIN**

characteristic	character, will
emotion	worry
element	Earth
organ	stomach
color	yellow
ages	early and late sixties, and early to midseventies

People don't follow their true path on their life's journey for many reasons; mostly they fear the disapproval of family and community. Imagine what it would be like to be born to an Amish family and want to be a race-car driver.

I met a man in New England years ago who was fifty-five years old with four grown children before he followed his heart and entered the priesthood. He had known his true calling since he was a child, but he didn't have a strong enough will to pursue it. When his family told him at nineteen that they had arranged a marriage for him with the daughter of a prominent family, he was too afraid of his father's anger and his mother's disappointment and embarrassment in their community to refuse. Not until his wife passed away did he consider fulfilling his vocation.

I noticed that he did have a rather small chin, and he had it covered with a goatee. I asked him how long he had worn it. "About a year after my wife died," he said. "And a year before I entered the order." When I told him the meaning of the chin in Taoism, he was impressed. He was astounded when I further told him that the ancient Taoist monks suggested growing a goatee to lengthen the chin to increase your will to live a long life according to your own terms.

Size and Shape

*The ancients believed that the ideal chin for a man
was prominent and squared, and for a woman,
oval and soft, but not passive.*

broad chin	strong-willed, confident, ambitious, honest, trouble expressing love, sensitive
square chin	idealist, strong-willed, sensible, straightforward
extremely square chin	high energy, combative, unforgiving, humorless, love luxury, demanding
extremely broad and large chin	tyrant
small chin	even-tempered, tolerant, easily influenced
very small chin	dreamy, creative, fantasy world, sensitive, easily influenced
round chin	friendly, generous, family-oriented, child-oriented
long chin	emotional, gamblers, energetic, affectionate
pointed chin	needs others, sensitive, fun, loves love, gossip, romantically adventurous
jutting chin	unusually healthy, very strong-willed
fleshy and turned-up chin	stubborn, passionate beliefs, friendly
straight chin	idealist

While the size of the chin tells us how much strength of character and will we have, the shape of the chin tells us about our temperament. A cooperative person usually has a wide, broad, or rounded chin, while argumentative and stubborn people tend to have angular, wedge-shaped chins.

A nice **broad chin** is great for business, but not so great for romance. These strong-willed, confident, ambitious, honest, and ethical people have trouble expressing love. They can love deeply and faithfully, but their relationships often fall

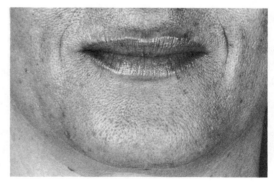

A broad chin

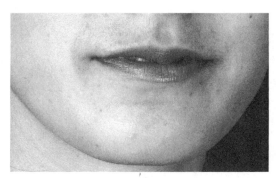

A slightly square chin

apart because they behave as though they're keeping their love a secret—from their loved ones especially. In both business and intimate relationships they are highly sensitive and will become vindictive if they think you have humiliated them in any way.

If you have a **square chin,** you are an idealist with a strong will and straightforward approach; you would make a great judge. People value you for your good sense and come to you for advice. Just be careful to let loose sometimes, especially in love.

Dick Tracy and most cartoon soldiers and warriors are depicted with **extremely square chins.** It's as though the illustrators knew the Taoist traits fit their characters so perfectly: high energy, combative, unforgiving, cannot deal with defeat or disrespect, and are more demanding than romantic in love. They love luxury, so much, in fact, that they can look the other way if it is ill-gotten. Arnold Schwarzenegger has a square chin, which fit his screen roles perfectly. It's gotten him in some trouble as governor, though.

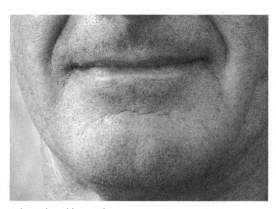

A broad and large chin

Those who have **extremely broad and large chins** are often tyrants. Think Rasputin and Saddam Hussein. These are the people who you hoped would have had small noses and cheekbones to balance out their outrageously strong wills.

Since people with **small chins** have to work harder to live life under their own terms, they can often turn out to be stronger, more willful, and more successful than those born with large chins. Remember, it's not simply having a gift or a challenge that determines your outcome in life; it is how you use it. With their even tempers and tolerance for the quirks in others, small-chinned people make great friends and teammates.

If you have a **very small chin** you certainly do have a challenge of finding your strength to lead your life according to your own terms. It doesn't mean you can't, only that you don't have the gift of easily standing up to those who oppose you. This is especially challenging since you do not respond well to feedback, even when it is helpful and warranted. Be careful not to construe all advice, direction, and disagreement as criticism. You have a great deal of creativity; channel it constructively. Don't get lost in your fantasies of how you wish your life could be; instead use that creativity to find healthy ways to pursue your goals. You can be tempted to lead someone else's life by being the loyal sidekick or helpmate. While these can be rewarding positions, be careful to also find your own path in life. Your life is a special gift, unique only to you. When you live your life through someone else, or you allow someone else to live your life, you can't help but be depressed, opening yourself to loneliness and even illness.

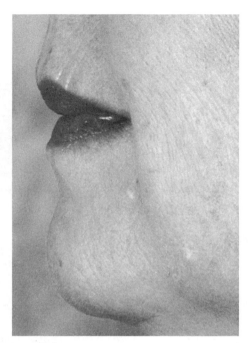

A small chin

Years ago I accompanied a theater director who was holding auditions in New York for the opera *La bohème*. The most convincing actresses for the role of Mimì all had **narrow chins,** the traits of which appropriately fit the character: sensitive, delicate, and uncertain. I was disappointed when the part was given to a woman with a wider chin but a well-known name. When I saw the opera on opening night, I realized what a great actress she was. She completely embodied the tragic character of Mimì, so much so that I swear her chin looked narrower.

When you need someone to listen to your problems and a warm shoulder to cry on, you go to people with a **round chin.** Their intuition is right on and you will do well to follow their generous advice.

First and foremost, they are family-oriented. Their quandary is that they choose their children over their spouse, creating resentful estrangements. The only

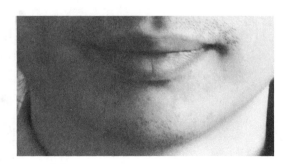

A round chin

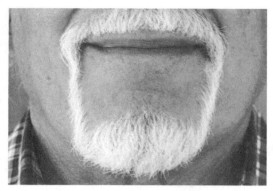

A long chin

time this works is if both parents have round chins; then they can unite in their doting.

Long-chinned people are seldom lonely. Their warmth and affectionate nature attract many loyal friends. They have a sincere concern for others, often getting emotional about those they care for. They are great teammates who are energetic, organized, and adventurous gamblers in work or play.

Comedian and late-night-television host Jay Leno has so much chin that he fits three Mien Shiang chin categories: long, broad, and rounded. He came to Hollywood to be a stand-up comedian but was told that he had a face "that would frighten children." Discouraged, he went into acting, auditioning for roles where it would be appropriate to frighten children. But he soon realized he needed to fight for his dreams, to live life according to his own terms. If anyone had enough chin to stand up for himself and his dreams, it was this man. He even titled his 1996 autobiography *Leading with My Chin*.

Pointed-chin people need to be around others. An evening alone can seem like eternity. Luckily they are incredibly friendly and social, attracting many friends and admirers. On the other hand, their love of gossip, their mood swings, and their overly sensitive nature threaten to make these relationships tentative and short-lived. These

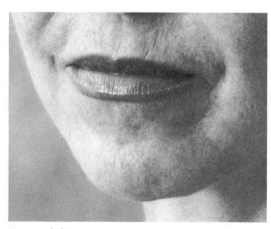

A pointed chin

people are excellent in businesses that require quick decision-making. Regrettably, they use this same skill in romance, quickly deciding that they have once again found the love of their life—but this time it's real! So in love with love are they, but they lack the staying power to have a fulfilling or long-lasting relationship, particularly in their youth. Even with therapy and guidance they have difficulty changing their impetuous overtures to friendship and romance. A shame, because they are so charming and fun and have much to offer. The good news is that by their late twenties or early thirties they do eventually find a true love to commit to. Then they will probably enjoy a long relationship, with the emphasis on love and fun.

It's said that if you have a **jutting chin,** you are very strong-willed and unusually healthy. I think that is because by extending your chin for the world to see, you are making a statement of rock-solid confidence in your abilities to live your life on your own terms. That in itself engenders a healthy mind, body, and spirit.

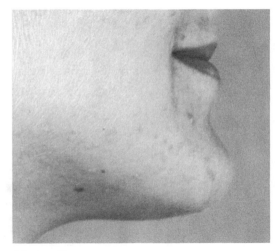
A jutting chin

Some people have nice padding on their chin, what we call a **fleshy chin.** And others have a little extra fatty tissue at the end of their chin that **turns up** slightly. Both the fleshy and the turned-up chin have the same outstanding trait: stubborness. Even more so, if that is possible, when the chin is both fleshy and turned up. I know several people with these chins, and it is great when we're on the same side of an argument, but aggravating when we are on opposite sides. They will not budge. What is satisfying, though, is that they argue their points and defend their positions with as much grace and kindness as passion; they are never insulting or rude.

An idealist most always has a **straight chin.** I taught a class last year in which one student had a long chin with a straight

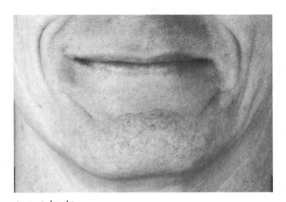
A straight chin

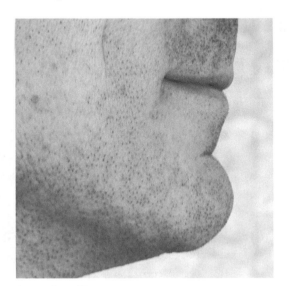
A turned-up chin

bottom, another had almost no chin at all but what was there was straight-edged, and a third had a narrow chin that was so straight it looked clipped. They all had varied personality traits matching their chin shapes other than straight, but at heart they were all idealists.

Markings on the Chin

REMINDER ABOUT FACIAL MARKINGS

Markings such as scars, lines, and some discolorations are acquired, while others, such as moles and birthmarks, can be inherited.

Markings on the left or right sides of the face reveal father's or mother's influence as well as your own inner or outer personality and behavior.

chin dimples	performers, funny, need attention, heightened emotions, sexual
cleft in chin	need lots of sexual attention, many passionate relationships
Starvation lines	starving for love and approval

If you have a **dimple** on your chin, you crave attention, and people love to give it to you because you're so fun and funny, even at the lowest of times. Flirting is an art for you, and your sexual nature is strong and rather entertaining. All of your emotions seem more heightened, and you cry easily—when you're happy, when you're sad, when you're excited, when you're passionate. You could never have a good relationship with someone who believes in the stiff-upper-lip theory of life.

A **cleft** in the chin is deeper and more prominent than a dimple, and so is the person's desire for attention and appreciation, especially if it is sexual. Frequently the person with the cleft chin has his or her feelings deeply hurt when the partner doesn't want intimacy all the time. Those with a cleft chin have difficulty separating the rejection of sex or intimacy, at that moment, from their partner's rejecting them forever. Somehow, they have mistakenly learned that physical love is the complete proof of emotional and spiritual love. They claim that this is the only time they feel truly cherished. Obviously, this can be painful if they are in constant fear of rejection. It's also painful for their mates, who feel they must perform in a specifically defined manner to demonstrate their love and feel rejected each time they try to express that love in other ways.

This constant need for assurance can lead to addictive behavior. In fact, I've been told by a member that if you want to see some good examples of cleft chins, head over to a sex addicts' meeting.

This is not to say that everyone with a cleft chin becomes addicted to sex. So don't start looking suspiciously at your mates or future dates. As with all of our natural challenges, many people with a cleft chin have learned to meet their innate challenge in myriad of ways. For instance, a high percentage of actors seem to have cleft chins. I think that the adoration of their public feeds their need for attention and appreciation to perfection, especially if they become sex idols. Also, I've seen lots of prosecuting attorneys, who are great performers in the courtroom, with cleft chins. Many have become superstars and enjoy much media fanfare and adulation from the public. I have also noticed that many actors who play courtroom attorneys on television have cleft chins!

In the section about Fa Ling lines we noted that sometimes the Fa Ling lines go down too low, making a circular line that connects under the chin. This, again, is called a **Starvation line** and belongs to someone who is starving for love and approval.

JAWS

determination fear Water kidney black/blue
late 70s to early 80s

Thousands of years ago the size and strength of our jaws determined how well we hunted and ate and how well we could protect ourselves. Nothing like a good pair of jaws when chowing down on leg of mastodon, or cracking the hard shells of nuts in search of a tasty morsel, or chasing off a predator who had his eye on your meal.

When I was a young girl living in New England, I remember a friend of my father's calling one of his employees "a real jawbone. That fella could talk to a lamppost and never get tired of the sound of his own voice." And he used to shake his head over the neighbors "jawing over nothing and coffee" every morning.

Jaw-dropping news is so amazing, surprising, unbelievable, or horrifying that you cannot even keep your lower mandible in place. Those slow on the uptake often look slack-jawed, and insults and anger can get you clench-jawed. Lockjawed is just a more down-home way of calling someone a snob.

The ancient Taoists had their own metaphor for the jaws; they called them "the roots of the tree of life." If our face is a map of our life's journey, then our jaws show if we are rooted in our beliefs.

Reading the jaws is a little different from the other facial features in that there are not as many different shapes and sizes as for eyes, noses, and mouths, for instance.

And though the shape and size of the jaw is read as a Water element, we sometimes consider the set of the jaw as a Wood element trait, especially if the set is communicating anger, frustration, or aggression. (A slack jaw, which represents passive behavior, wouldn't, therefore, be considered a positive Wood element trait, but rather a deficient Wood trait.)

ALWAYS CONSIDER THE **WATER ELEMENT** ASSOCIATIONS FOR THE **JAWS**

characteristic	determination
emotion	fear
element	Water
organ	kidney
color	black/blue
ages	late seventies to early eighties

Size and Shape

large, broad, or prominent jaws	determined, will fight for self and for beliefs, honorable
small or narrow jaws	easily swayed by arguments and emotions

Large, broad, or prominent jaws all indicate that we are willing to fight for ourselves and for what we believe. A little reminder to our prominent-jawed friends: Just because you believe something does not make it true. And just because someone does not share your beliefs does not make them wrong. Since you are by nature honorable, keep that at hand when you come upon opposition. Use your gift of determi-

A broad jaw

A prominent jaw

nation to help you create responsibility and fairness when you take your strong stand in the world.

If you have **small or narrow jaws,** you have to stay focused on knowing yourself, believing in yourself, and holding your ground. Your challenge is to not get swept up in others' causes, ignoring your own needs. If you find you are easily swayed by others' arguments and emotions, give yourself plenty of alone time to meditate, and to analyze the issues or feelings, before you make a decision.

Former president Bill Clinton was known for driving his Secret Service agents and advisers mad because he would stop to talk with anyone, any-

A narrow jaw

time, always eager to hear another point of view or opinion. It makes sense if you take a look at his **narrow jaws.** Even as president of a powerful country, he did not have the natural gift of conviction and needed to seek others' views before he made crucial decisions. His wife, on the other hand, has very determined jaws; she is known for making quick, sure decisions. I imagine that this is what has made them an effective team over the years, complementing each other's challenges. Or, as I like to say, he married the jaws and she married the chin.

Set of the Jaws

clenched jaws	angry, tense
slack-jawed	confused, puzzled, uncomprehending
dropped jaw	surprised, amazed, puzzled, uncertain, disbelieving, horrified

The set of the jaw can be chronic or fleeting depending on each new set of emotions. When people have chronically **clenched** jaws, it is because they are continually angry and tense. This excess Wood element trait probably shows elsewhere on the face, especially in the intense set and stare of the eyes, as well as the muscles around the eyes, and in eyebrows and the Yin Tong area.

Those who are habitually **slack-jawed** are not generally quick-witted or quick to comprehend the vagaries of most situations. They need guidance and patience in most areas of their lives.

Jaw-dropping events happen to all of us periodically, for reasons from great to horrifying. It's hard to imagine someone continuously surprised, amazed, puzzled, uncertain, disbelieving, or horrified, so it's safe to say that the dropped jaw is transient. Of course, for some their everyday life is a bit of ongoing street theater, and the dropped jaw is a great facial prop for their performances.

AFTERWORD

IN THE BEGINNING OF THIS book I stated that the search for self-discovery is a powerful and universal quest. Unfortunately, I have found that too many of us consider this search for self as a path to becoming someone else—a perfect version of our dream selves. We can be so hard on ourselves, feeling shame, disappointment, or even self-loathing, when we cannot eliminate or control our "big" emotions such as anger, obsession, worry, grief, or fear.

I sincerely hope that the Tao of Mien Shiang has helped you to see that each of us comes into the world with innate gifts and challenges, and that these very gifts and challenges are reflected on our faces. If you look in the mirror and see prominent brow bones, I hope you will be thankful for the gift as well as the challenge of your issue with control. If you see strong cheekbones, I hope you will be aware of the challenge of your authority as well as appreciative of the gift.

As you more clearly understand and accept your true nature, you will also appreciate the true natures of others. It's a great relief to realize by your mate's thick eyebrows that his difficulty in controlling anger is not about you or your relationship, but that anger is his innate challenge in life (his gift, too). Once you remove yourself from engaging in his anger, you can even help him to see its source and to understand that he can change his attitude, behavior, and thoughts about his use of anger.

And it's good to know that your coworker with the tiny ears keeps rejecting your proposals to move boldly forward because she is by nature not a risk-taker, not because she doesn't trust or appreciate your vision. You can expend your energy reassuring her rather than resenting her.

Mien Shiang can give you the insights and knowledge to make your life richer, happier, and more profound in every way. I wish you much love, happiness, and adventure as you continue your life's journey.

ACKNOWLEDGMENTS

I AM DEEPLY INDEBTED TO so many people for the creation of this book.

Heartfelt thanks to my agent, my friend Bonnie Solow, for seeing the book in Mien Shiang and for guiding me every step of the way. And appreciation to Mary Palisoul, who so beautifully helped Bonnie help me.

My experience with all the good people at Dutton has been outstanding. Brian Tart, my brilliant editor, is literally a dream come true. The talented, supportive Neil Gordon made every suggestion and edit a pleasure. Beth Parker's enthusiasm and encouragement is very appreciated.

In Tucson, Kresta King Cutcher, Belinda Berry, and Barbara Isaacson kept me on track with expertise and care. Henry J. Lee, at the end, pulled it all together in Santa Monica; I could not have done it without him. Thank you all.

I am grateful to all of my many exceptional students, especially to Jay Bulloch, Jin Kyoung Jun, and Yong-bin Yuk, for being my cheerleaders and eventually my friends over the years. The same for Veronique Vial, photographer extraordinaire, who holds the record for attending the most Mien Shiang workshops, and who with the equally generous Philip Dixon has numerous times provided a beautiful and loving space for me to teach in.

Dr. Maoshing Ni, Dr. Daoshing Ni, and Sum Yee Wang brought me in to Yo San University of Traditional Chinese Medicine to create the first certificate program in Mien Shiang. That was my first step in writing this book, and for that I will be forever appreciative.

Ivy Ross introduced me and Mien Shiang to the corporate world. I will always be grateful for her foresight, brilliance, and most especially for her friendship.

A bow to Robbie Long for the walks and talks, years of friendship, and belief in the Mien Shiang book, and for leading me to Bonnie; and to Bidhan Roy, who early on prodded me to write this book. Thanks for the insight and the laughs and for getting past the tough times. He is, and he deserves, Joy.

Brian Flagg of Casa Maria, whose commitment to fighting the good fight continues to inspire me to make a difference.

Christian Morrow reminds me to teach, to challenge, to accept, to grow, and to enjoy.

And last, but always first, thanks and love to Elliot Munjack, M.D. It could not have happened without his love and belief.

NOTE: The photographs throughout this book were taken by Nassim Khakpour, with the exception of the photo on page 90, which was taken by Fred Fox Studios, Chicago, Illinois.

Each beautiful face belongs to a friend, student, or neighbor. Thank you all for your generosity. It's hard to describe the joy of having you be part of this journey.

LA PHOTO MODELS:

Cameron Aston, Fiora Aston, Linton Bergsen, Travor Boehm, Jay Bulloch, JoAnne Cerenzio, Richard Cerenzio, Joy Cloud, Tiffani Corral, Laraine Crampton, Keiko Cronin, Raymond Daniels, Alisa Dennis, Michael Edelstein, Cofe Vidze Fiakpui, Genevieve Fong, Dawn Fortunato, Lyndon Gardner, Richard Goss, Linda Gross, Lynde Hartman, Peter Helenek, Daria Hines, Bill Hogan, Derek Hubbard, Karin Huebner, Jin Jun, Jeanne Kane, Dianne Lange, Henry Lee, Dennis Manuel, Meryl Marshall, Richard Mattingly, Montana McGlynn, Lisa Milillo, Michael Milillo, Darien Morea, Donna Morton, Elliot Munjack, Janet Nelson, Ian Ng, Tracy Ng,

Kimberly Reid, Denise Riley, Bidhan Roy, Foster Ryan, Kathryn Schorr, Bernadette Styburski, Edsel Tan, Hilary Taub, Kara Taub, Scott VanOpdorp, Dia Vickery, Yong-bin Yuk.

TUCSON PHOTO MODELS:
David Scott Allen, Belinda Berry, Oscar Boycrguez, Laura Brynwood, Connie Carter, Jefferson Carter, Evo DeConcini, Satoko DeConcini, Brian Flagg, Kate Garner, Paul Gohdes, Dolores Gohdes, Felipe Jara Gomeli, Nancy Hand, Rich Hopkins, Gina Inman, Barbara Isaacson, Buzz Isaacson, Ike Isaacson, Raena Isaacson, Jorge Morales, Mimi Kurtin, Annie Lewis, Francisco Javier Mazon, Pancho Medina, Rolando Medina, Jon Miles, Cynthia Miller (Chicago), Nancy Myers, Maria Neagle, Erika O'Dowd, Manuela Irma Ortiz, Kevin Pakulis, Josh Pope, Marianne Ritter, Adrianna Rodriguez, Anthony Rodriguez, Betsy Rollings, Mark Sammons, Ken Shackman, Lin Shackman, Jerry Skalet, Maria del Carmen Tautimez, Barbie Urias, Maryada Vallet, Father John Williamson.

Patrician McCarthy is the first Mien Shiang expert to translate this ancient science for the mainstream American public. For over twenty years, she has taught medical students, alternative health practitioners, lawyers, Olympic athletes, and corporate CEOs from Procter & Gamble Co., Mattel Inc., Old Navy, and The Gap the powerful implications of face reading. She founded the Mien Shiang Institute and, in conjunction with the renowned Yo San University of Traditional Chinese Medicine in Los Angeles, established the first certificate program in Mien Shiang. She lives in California and Arizona. This is her first book.